In the Name of Peace

A Country Called the World

Mehdi Seifi Kebriya

Translated by, Piter Saloon

A Country Called the World

A Country Called the World

Book Title: A Country Called the World

Author: Mehdi Seifi Karbiya

Translator (from Persian): Piter Saloon

Cover design: Shima Izadbakhsh

Publisher: Supreme Century, USA

ISBN: 978-1939123831

A Country Called the World

Content:

A Country Called the World

A Country Called the World

Iran

Under the Carpet

The letter was written with the simplest words and many misspellings,

"High, dear lady. I want to tell you there ease a man who loves you so much and is prepared to satisfy your every wish. I was alone for years, and during this time, whenever I thought about myself, I remembered an old and worn out carpet, weaved with the worst quality yarn, and although it belongs to the house floor, people rather spread it on pebbles and walk on it with soiled and dirty shoes. But when I saw you, I felt like I was a carpet in the royal palace, woven from the very best of yarns and never wears out. I will soon send you another letter. Goodbye."

Shortly after reading the letter, when Mahshid got up to turn the kitchen light off, she noticed that, as usual, her daughter had fallen asleep next to the heater while doing her school homework. She lifted her slowly in her arms and took her to the bedroom and after she returned to the heater to put her book and notebook in the bag, she noticed that her daughter's handwriting is like the handwriting that had written the letter, and as she inspected it more carefully, she could not see any difference between them. She thought that there was no reason for her daughter, Thermae, to write that letter. In fact, the handwriting of all the kids of the same age are similar and maybe the letter was written by the same boy who brought the letter to her. What's more, Mahshid had long felt that her neighbor was interested in her. Her neighbor was a man who lived even more isolated than Mahshid. He had separated from his wife and lost his only child after divorce. Mahshid and the man smiled when they occasionally met each other. Mahshid, in a conversation they had in the past, had told him that she had lost her husband when Thermae was one-year-old. The neighbor man, after Mahshid finished her story, had said, 'What a coincidence! What a difference! While we are both lonely, at the same time, the type of our loneliness is different.' However, Mahshid and the man next door had a friendly relationship and it was still a short time since they had become neighbors and met each other.

In bed, Mahshid was thinking, 'Perchance, he will show me his love me a bit later. Maybe he loves me. Sure he does! But, why he has written such a letter, while we see each other almost every day? He is educated, so why should he write such a letter and send it out anonymously like this? It is ridiculous that someone compares oneself with a carpet! Why carpet?' Shortly afterward, due to sleepiness, the letter incident faded out in her mind. She hugged her daughter and fell asleep.

The next morning, after taking her daughter to school, she went to work. Often, during the four years that she worked in a laundry service, she tried to get busy with her work to keep away from paranoid thoughts. But that day, no matter how much she tried to keep her mind engaged, she just could not help to forget that she had received a love letter. She hoped that none other than the man next door had sent the letter because Mahshid liked him, but she had not noticed this deep interest until the time she felt like to attribute the letter to him. That long black hair and elongated dim brown eyes only belonged to the man next door, and if Mahshid was going to fall for someone he was the obvious option. She wore her black top and shorts only for his eyes, to emphasize her mesmerizing round bosoms and figure and her smooth, white tummy.

"He must be shy. Yeah! It is him. He showed me his love so naughtily, like the kids! How discreet! How different!"

She naively felt good by the thought that someone was going to save her from loneliness. Someone who had a troubled life like her. But she concealed her happiness because the laundry service owner would become cheeky if he saw her like that. He was a middle-aged and lewd man; he flirted with numerous girls although he had a wife and a couple of children. Mahshid had no problem if the boy who had brought the letter had written it too, but could not imagine at all that the letter might have been sent by the owner of the laundry service.

At lunch, she changed her work clothes to go after her daughter as usual and take her home. As she stepped out of the laundry, the shop owner arrived. He took out his hands from the pockets of his coat, squeezed the back of his neck - which was not clear that it was white with red spots or red with white spots - and said, "Are you going for your daughter?"

Mahshid, "Yes. Goodbye."

The shop owner, "Wait!"

He looked inside the shop and said, "There. Put the shirt that has fallen to the floor, on the table. Then go."

Mahshid returned to the shop, and first tried to pick up the shirt off the ground with her foot, but when she realized it was impossible, she bent over back to the wall and picked it from the floor. The shop owner, like a vulture whose prey suddenly comes back to life and flees, angrily entered the shop after Mahshid's departure.

Mahshid took her daughter home and, after making lunch for her, returned to the laundry service. The shop owner was gone.

She had finished all the work and the clothes they had received yesterday and the day before that were ready. She glanced at the clock, and while yawning, went toward the tall stool at the corner. A comfortable chair was near the table, but she preferred the stool, perhaps because the shop owner usually sat on that chair. Her eyes were heavy with sleep. She turned down the sound of the radio beside her on the metal niche and leaned her head to the wall. She took a nap for ten minutes and then got up. She felt well, she did not feel like sleeping anymore but she was hungry. It was 2 PM, and she had to stay at the shop for another two hours. After twenty minutes, a customer came in and collected his clothes. He was the fifth customer since morning. A bit later, a woman came in and submitted the graduation gown of her first child to the laundry, so she could use them within two days when her child was supposed to graduate. Mahshid felt unhappy unwittingly. She told herself how lucky she was because she had just one child! After all, customers collected their clothes and some people brought their clothes to her and the working hours of Mahshid ended, the boy who had given her the letter on the previous day entered the shop. Mahshid looked at the women's apparel in his hand. It was a long robe that was usually worn by old ladies. The boy had thrown down his hammer-like head – which had surely provoked his schoolmates to sarcastically call him two-headed– and looked stealthily at Mahshid.

A Country Called the World

He said with a shaky voice, "My grandmother will come tomorrow to collect it."

He put the robe on the counter, and before he had a chance to leave a letter on the dress and quickly run away, Mahshid grasped his hand and asked, "Who sent this letter?"

The boy was afraid, but being an enfant terrible, he tried to free himself from Mahshid's grip.

Mahshid firmly held his shoulders to keep him in place. Abruptly, she asked the boy loudly, "How old are you? Do you know reading and writing?"

She realized the boy was going to burst into tears. So, she let go of him to avoid attracting the attention of shopkeepers who ogled her all the time. When she closed the shop and arrived home, she saw the man next door who had just arrived home and was busy finding the key to his house. The neighbor man greeted Mahshid casually and Mahshid replied with a smile. In a fleeting moment, she decided to ask him whether he had sent the letter, but she regretted it. It was just impossible that the neighbor man would do such a foolish thing.

Mahshid decided not to read the letter and throw it away, but she thought perhaps the sender might have introduced himself this time. In any case, if the letter was not from the man next door which she was sure that it was not - she would throw it away. The letter was written in the same style, but this time it seemed to be written in a hurry,

"Hello, dear lady. Dear Mahshid! Forgive my boldness for calling you by your first name. If you agree to meet each other, give the letter's reply to the same boy who brought you the letter. Do not worry. He is a smart boy. I told him to give you the letter whenever you are alone. Goodbye. I love you."

Mahshid threw away the letter and vowed if she would see the boy in the shop again, twist his tiny ear that was stuck to his head, and look up his parents.

The next morning, one hour after she took her daughter to the school, she remembered that she had forgotten to put the meal in her bag. So, she immediately returned home and picked the bread and cheese that were wrapped in a plastic bag from the table and went to the school.

By the time she reached the school, it was the break time. She did not have the time to look for her daughter. She decided to go to the principal's office so they summon her daughter via the public address speaker system, but she gave up the idea. Something caught her eye. She went to the corner of the yard. Her daughter was sitting on the stairs of the school custodian's quarters beside the custodian and was busy writing. Mahshid could realize from that angle that a scrap pickup van that was parked in the yard blocked the line of sight from the principal's office to the custodian's home.

The school custodian and Thermae did not notice Mahshid was standing a few feet away, watching them carefully. When Mahshid stepped closer, the school custodian saw her and jumped to his feet anxiously. Mahshid daughter's head was down, so she did not notice her mother was approaching.

She said, "OK, I wrote the *I* ! I what, uncle Siavash?" and her eyes fell on Mahshid, and then she walked to her mother dubiously if she was caught red-handed. Mahshid hugged her.

A Country Called the World

The old man, who was still ogling Mahshid, said with embarrassment, "I am Siavash. The custodian of your daughter's school. Your admirer."

Mahshid turned her glowering eyes away from the school's custodian and looked inside his home whose door was left open. She saw the carpet in his room which as he had described previously, was jaded and worn out. She wished she had the power to crush the old man, his home and pick up van between her two fingers, like tiny snails that she used to pick up and hold them in her palm, and after great patience, she crushed them when they emerged from their shell. But she did not do anything, and after a brief pause, as she had Thermae in her arms, exited the school; indifferent to her 'Where do we go? Where do we go?'.

Moments after Mahshid's departure, the school custodian went inside, pushed the carpet aside and held the picture of his deceased wife - which he had taken out of its frame sometime in the past and sneaked it under the carpet - close to his chest and shed tears.

A Country Called the World

A Country Called the World

The United States of America

The Sound of Silence

Richard was one of the few soldiers who survived the last battalion of American soldiers arriving in Italy. When he returned from the war, he was mostly into himself, and although he was maimed, suffered shell shock, and occasionally a lot of noise twirled in his head, but he never regretted going to war. Unlike him, his comrades who returned from the war, talked about their memories to everyone, both to their family and relatives and strangers and even to each other. Memories that seemed endless and each time they were narrated, they were still fresh and even with the passage of time, when there were less eager ears to hear them, no exaggeration was involved in their retelling. Of course, the speaker, not willing to hurt anyone, but just because the events that he witnessed in the war were so horrible that the mind was unable to imagine and he felt they seemed immensely weird to a person who had not experienced them; described what he had seen in full detail.

Richard was not interested in speaking about what he had experienced in the war, neither in his youth nor at old age, unlike many old men who in their gatherings, directed the discussion in a way that they would be the only speaker in the meeting, so they could talk about their memories.

However, a few years passed since he was maimed, and then, he was a 70-year-old man who spent his days in his humble home in California with two arms amputated from the elbow. He returned all of his medals and military uniforms to the organization shortly after recovery. He did not attend any ceremonies related to him or other military personnel, and even after he was discharged from the hospital, every month he transferred sixty percent of the pension that they had allocated to him to a charity account.

It was the early days of the spring. Richard was rocking to and fro next to the window on an old rocking chair whose cracks under its legs looked like the cracks on his soles and enjoyed the landscape. The sunlight cast right over his face, but it did not hurt the old man.

With a smile on his lip that made his face look sadder, he told his sitter that it would be better to turn off the phonograph so that the house atmosphere would be filled solely with the sound of sparrows on the tree. The sparrows on the tree were so numerous that they looked like its produce and fruits. It was a long time that the sitter had become indifferent to the old man's cheerfulness and his happy hours, because she had realized Richard was usually happy like idiots, and the soft nature sounds or the construction workers' noise had no impact on him at all.

As usual, he had been waiting for William, his brother's grandson, to arrive and shave his face. Richard was particularly interested in him. The sitter put the shaver, shaving crème, towel, and mirror at hand. When Richard glanced at the watch for the second time on that morning, William entered the house and put down his backpack and after a military salute to Richard, immediately picked up the shaving crème and started his job. He was in a hurry because he had to report to the garrison at nine thirty. Richard replied his military salute with a grim face and looked at him as a captive.

A Country Called the World

William raised his head vigorously and said, "What is your opinion about private William Clooney, the ace of the US Army?!"

Richard impatiently glanced at the shaving crème.

Brian said, "Yes, sir!" and after turning the phonograph on, started to rhythmically apply the crème to Richard's face.

When the shaving was nearly over, Richard murmured sarcastically, "So, you finally got yourself into the military!"

William, "I have been a military man since childhood! Last night, I was looking at the signatures that I used to put under my books and notebooks at the age of nine, 'Colonel William Clooney'! Oh! I have to hurry. I must report to the garrison within half an hour, otherwise, my name goes into the list of cowards!"

Richard, "What is so wonderful in a war that attracts you?"

William, "I do not get the satisfaction I feel in this uniform elsewhere. What in the world is better than fighting for the homeland? No one can serve his country as a military man serves his country."

The young sitter glanced hatefully at William's backpack and asked Richard for a one-hour leave to take her child who had caught a cold to the doctor. Richard permitted her to go and told her to get him a newspaper on the way back.

Richard, "You never asked me why I signed up in the army. Why did I go to war?"

William replied immediately, "It is crystal clear to me that you entered the army for the love of your homeland."

A Country Called the World

He wiped Richard's face with the towel and held the mirror in front of him.

Richard checked himself and said, "I'm getting old!" and sent a kiss to himself which made William laugh.

William took a few steps back and saluted again and picked up his bag and said, "I will never allow the right to be trampled. I will capture Giáp[1] all on my own! Farewell!"

Richard said with a serious tone, "Wait, William. There is still time. I will not waste too much of your time. You do not know anything about me except for my age, my position on the front, the battalion in which I was serving, and how I lost my arms? Do you?"

William, "Well, is there any other important thing that was not said besides this?"

Richard, "The reason for my going to war! I never told you the reason for my departure. I was not supposed to say it either. But now, when I see the veins of your neck are so thunderously swelled for the homeland, I have to tell you the reason for my going to war. I did not go to war for the love of my homeland."

William let go of the door handle, and his desperate look at Richard told him that he was eager to hear what he had to say. Were there any more sacred and obvious reasons to go to war than to serve the homeland? He encouraged himself that perhaps Richard had a reason superior to what he had seen in himself up to that moment, but the possibility that the grandfather had gone to war because of ambition, to attain high positions and being respected, easily swallowed his optimism.

---

[1] Võ Nguyên Giáp (1911-2013). Vietnam military minister and chief of staff.

A Country Called the World

Richard said after a brief pause, "Up to twenty-nine days before I went to the army, I had a mistress by the name Stephanie, a skinny and beautiful girl who never let us listen to music when we were alone.

"The first time she came to our home and we were supposed to have dinner together, I wanted to turn on the gramophone, but she disagreed and said, "Music will make the moments between us eternal. It is not good at all if there is a day that we have to part for any reason, we remember each other by listening to that song and suffer a lot. Let's not get rid of the silence!" So, we never listened to music whenever we were alone. Indeed, the climax of our happy moments was when we spent time in silence.

On a November night, when the gypsy carnival set up its tent in our village, I and she walked there slowly, hand in hand. Clearly, the music was forbidden only in a place where nobody was present except us, and this law did not apply to parties. Wow, what a feast and celebration! A fire eater swallowed fire, a clown did amazing bicycle tricks, another one walked the rope blindfolded, and a young lady dancer entertained everyone. Everything was awesome, but to me, it was not so attractive. I longed to be alone with Stephanie ASAP. Indeed, nothing was sweeter than the silence that Stephanie had established between us. She was well aware of my interest in that kind of silence. The cold weather began to pour gradually. When the rain became more intense, the gypsies wound up their acts and the people rushed home. But we were happy, and the rainy weather did not have any impact on us. Under the rain, I ran toward home following her. Before we reach the house, I was constantly reaching for her and she laughed and escaped my grasp. Oh! We were near home when the lightning struck and she screamed and turned to me to take refuge in me, but at that time, I escaped from her. The next day, when I went to their home, her mother was sitting sadly in her room. Stephanie's face was pale and she had a high fever. Her mother, before she gave me a dirty look and go out of the room, said that the doctor had been there a few minutes ago and warned her never let her daughter go outdoors in cold weather. A deep silence prevailed in the house and no sound was heard except the barking of a dog in the distance. I was sure nobody could hear the barking other than me. I felt that I needed to hear a sound because the silence was terribly annoying. So, I did not know whether I was really hearing the dog's barking or it was just my imagination. Stephanie was asleep. I saw their housekeeper and asked whether Stephanie's situation had gotten worse just in the previous night. She said, "Yes, but if her mother did not notice she was going down, nobody could figure out that she was ill. Even the slightest moan was not heard from Stephanie's throat." I thought to myself maybe she was worried about her family noticing it and put the blame on me, so, she had tried to hide her illness from everyone. Stephanie! (Richard called out her name with a long sigh and stopped talking for a few moments).

"She died two weeks later. No matter how I tried to convince myself that the silence that engulfed my loneliness after her death was different than the silence I had experienced with Stephanie, I could not do it. A terrible silence! You cannot imagine the torment I suffered from the sound of silence after Stephanie's death. I was teetering at the edge of madness. I could feel her every time I was alone. I saw her in front of me. I felt she was waiting for me somewhere near me. Once, when I was alone at home, sitting in my room, I felt that she was in the living room, and when I got up and went to the living room,

A Country Called the World

I felt that she was standing in the hall, and so on from the hall to the kitchen, to my parents' room and other rooms, in the yard, and then I returned to my room! It was both scary and tortuous. I used to sleepwalk quite a few times because her whisper was calling me and I went out of the house. If my parents did not notice, it was not clear where I would end up. Believe me, I talked to her many times and even patted her hair! And when I realized that she was not real but living in my imagination and I was actually talking to myself, I panicked and looked around lest someone could see me. One day, I noticed that I had been addicted deeply to my daydreaming and it had been a while that I was living with her in paranoia, and that was why I was deserted and alone; and also I realized that everyone doubted my sanity. Afterward, I could not keep her away from me, no matter how hard I tried. Whenever I was in silence, she began to talk, 'It seems that you do not like me anymore! I am alive! You are seeing me! Why do not you believe me!' That was her! She was there! It was a force that, even if I wanted to, would not allow me to leave my privacy and mingle with the crowd and spend good times with my friends like before. But one day I finally managed to go to a party of a friend of mine. In that place, she did not come to me anymore! I no longer saw her and I did not hear her voice as well. After that party, I always escaped silence; I turned on the gramophone when I was alone, I was mostly in the crowd, I was usually drunk, and even slept with the sound of the gramophone. However, silence found a way to come to me. When I woke up, for a few seconds, as I walked toward the gramophone to turn it on, silence attacked me and I remembered Stephanie. And anyway, for how long could I go on drinking wine, stay in the crowd, and sing and listen to the music? I decided to eliminate the silence by any means.

"Twenty-nine days after Stephanie's death, I entered the army, and I went to war shortly afterward. The sound of bullets, burst fire, mortars and grenades, an explosion had destroyed the silence. There was so much ruckus that it was unbelievable to imagine there was silence in the world, too. As if silence never existed at all from the beginning. All of the soldiers were disturbed and anxious, but I fought the enemy with laughter. The commander and the soldiers thought that I had lost my mind. I was happy because silence was not there! After a few hours of fighting, we defeated them, and you know the rest of the story."

Richard glanced at his non-existent hands. As if he had formed them into a fist in his imagination. While he was speaking, there was no trace of discomfort in his face. William was staring at Richard's mouth.

Richard, "After the mine blast, a ringing sound stayed put in my head forever. Silence?! All but gone!"

William was speechless. The clock showed it was 10 AM.

A Country Called the World

Chile

The Terrible Mask

Isabel was not the oldest person in the village, but she felt her death was close at hand. However, she did not take the feeling seriously. But that feeling really scared her one day when she woke up late and realized her soul has entered into her body with a delay, unlike the past days. From that day on, she began to think about how she would die. She did not want to die in her sleep.

Therefore, one day she went to meet her friend Martha at her home, and told her, "I want to die in Atacama[2]."

Martha was unsuccessfully trying to cut in half a coconut she held in her hand, so she called her grandson, "Exactly half! Look, boy, I myself could have cut it like that if I wanted to."

Without looking at her grandson, who was a heavyset boy, she snatched the coconut shell that had been broken into three unequal pieces from his hand, and addressed Isabel, "I think these two pieces are equal to this one. Aren't they?"

To divert her friend's attention to coconut, Isabel immediately took the two pieces from her hand which were not equal at all and said, "They are exactly the same!" and proceed to eat them and asked, "Where would you like to die?"

Martha glanced at her for a moment and said, "From this distance that I am checking them, I see they are not equal and

---

[2] A desert with an area of 105,000 square kilometers, located between Chile, Peru, and Bolivia.

your coconut is smaller than my coconut. Much smaller! Give it to me. Believe me; I do not agree that. . . did you nibble on both pieces?"

When she noticed that Isabel is eating the coconut indifferent to her concern, she also took a bite into her coconut softly and indecisively. Isabel thought that perhaps her friend, that seventy-year-old cheerful woman, does not like to talk about death. She seemed to be very bold in the sense that she easily talked about death. It was not unusual for the people of her age to think about death, but they did not like to talk about it, just like middle-aged people who think about aging but do not want to talk about it.

Martha said after a brief pause, "Death! Death! Death! How old do you think you are? Just eighty-two years, which is not the time to die. "

Isabel, "But I feel it."

Martha said, "Aha, perhaps it is because of the story you made up? That is, you were sleeping and your soul saw your body asleep and. . ." She ended with a smiled.

Isabel, "Have you experienced this feeling too?"

Martha, "Frequently! The last time was yesterday night; my soul was not going to return to my body."

Isabel, "Were not you scared?"

Martha, "Of course I freaked out. But let me reassure you! What was the name of the husband of your aunt's daughter? Aha, Isaac! I will not die until I break the record of old Isaac."

Isabel, "He is a hundred and five!"

Martha, "And still alive!"

A Country Called the World

Isabel, "I hope you live longer than him. Look, I would love to die in the Atacama."

Martha, "You mean you like to be taken there while you are dying?"

Isabel, "No, I want to go to the Atacama while I am still alive and keep on walking till I die. When I am supposed to die and no longer have the stamina to live and work, does it make any difference how I die? I want to choose my own type of death by myself."

Martha laughed madly and said, "You, foxy little bitches! So the people would say she died due to the fatigue of desert trekking, not because of aging!"

Isabel smiled, "Maybe!"

Isabel and all the people of her age knew that if they received the slightest respect from the youth and people younger than their age, it was solely because of their white hair and wrinkly face. However, among their own age group, especially those who, like Isabel and her friends, had a good or moderate scientific standing, nothing was worse than receiving such respect from the people who were unaware of their position in the past. Rarely anyone who pays respect to old people is aware of the fact that one day they have been teachers, university professors, capitalists, physicians, con artists or... ., especially if they are all in a nursing home. Anyway, even if their standing was supposed to be accounted for, the first thing that caught the eye and aroused respect was nothing other than their white hair and squeezed faces. So, Isabel and her comrades did not take such respect too seriously and tried to do most of their work on their own.

A Country Called the World

Isabel packed a piece of bread, a piece of coconut, and two water bottles in a two-layered cloth bag that she had already sewn. Then, like a gladiator who puts on his armor a few minutes before the fight and with the sword in hand, imagines himself fighting against a diehard opponent, stood on the porch and looked at the Atacama. She could even imagine at what spot of Atacama she will die. It was dawn, and her daughter, son in law, three grandchildren, and five great-grandchildren, all of whom lived in her large house, was asleep. Isabel saw Isaac while descending the wooden staircase. Isaac's house was next to Isabel's house. At that time in the morning, Isaac was also sitting on the porch of his home and looked at the Atacama. He was very proud because he was the oldest one of them and received the most respect, although in his younger days he was a cunning thief. The generation that had witnessed his robberies was no longer there and only Isabel and two women older than her remembered his robberies. In her childhood, Isabel saw Isaac stole a lamb from her father's flock and fled. No one saw him except Isabel, and Isaac was unaware that Isabel had seen him. Isabel was very fond of that lamb, but could not tell the father that she knew who the thief was, because Isaac would have lost face and might have been punished hard. From that very day, Isabel never spoke to Isaac again. But when she grasped the railing and started to descend the stairs as if she was walking on highly delicate golden chains rather than rough wood, she spoke softly to Isaac.

- "I saw that you stole my lamb. I do not want to remind you of the past. I just wanted to tell you why I was not on speaking terms with you. Not a big deal. I forgave you forever."

Isaac did not show any reaction, but in the moonlight twilight, Isabel imagined that Isaac nodded and smiled.

A Country Called the World

When the sun lit up everywhere, Isabel's daughter along with her youngest great-grandchild went downstairs to go to the bathroom and saw Isaac there. If Isabel's daughter woke up a little earlier, she would have surely noticed the black spot that was moving in the desert. Isaac, lying on his side and holding his half-clenched hands on his legs which were a result of stroke a few years ago, was staring ahead. Isabel's daughter thought it would be better to notify her mother, so she would tell her aunt's daughter about Isaac's death. When she noticed Isabel was not in her room, she went to the kitchen to kiss her face as usual, and this time, before having her prepared breakfast, inform her about Isaac's death. But later, when she found out that her mother was not home, she started to worry. It was unusual for Isabel to leave home before she woke up. She said to herself, "Maybe, she is at Martha's."

Then she went inside Isaac's house to inform his wife but she was not home either. A moment after she entered Isaac's house, she saw his wife, children, grandchildren, great-grandchildren, twice great-grandchildren, and thrice great-grandchildren that were approaching her house. Their number was so many that Isaac could easily set up an empire using them.

A few minutes before, Isaac's wife, Marcela, after she realized her husband was dead, sat next to him and tried hard to weep for him but could not do so. She was extremely aged. Her eyes could do nothing but blurring the vision. She was so old that she could hardly show any feelings. No matter how hard she tried to show her discomfort, she was unsuccessful. Her voice had become sore long before Isaac's death and could hardly be heard and the trembling of her hands and head also had nothing to do with Isaac's death. Finally, in the presence of her children, she had to do what she had done before at the funeral of some of

27

her friends and repeatedly hit her head hard. Her oldest child took her hands and consoled her. As a matter of fact, her children knew that the one who was more upset than them was no one except Marcela, their mother. But Marcela thought her children suspected she was not so happy about Isaac or she was so heartless that she would not shed any tears for him.

After two days from Isaac's death and disappearance of Isabel, Martha invited her friends to her home and held a meeting. The friends consisted of Marcela, a very white woman named Alice and the triplet sisters who always carried a similar case and bracelet, but their dress style was not the same from their younger days till the moment of death.

The fact was that Martha did not take what Isabel had told her a few days ago seriously at all, but two days ago, Isabel's daughter asked her about her mother. Martha liked what Isabel had done, but she was afraid to do it alone. So, she asked her friends, "Is there anyone among you who wants to choose the type of her death?" The friends exchanged glances and one of the triplet sisters said, "I thought we were going to talk about Isabel's disappearance."

Martha replied, "We will get to it later."

The other one said, "I did not get it. Explain further."

Martha, "We all know that death is not far from us. My question is simple. Do you want to die of aging? Marcela, I apologize you. Do you like when you die, the reason for your death, like that of her husband, is old age?"

All were silent and stared at Martha's mouth to suggest a solution, but they noticed that Marcela was talking.

Martha, "I did not understand. What did Marcela say, Alice?"

A Country Called the World

Alice, "She said 'do we have any other choice'?"

Martha, "Isabel went to the Atacama."

Alice, "When?"

Martha, "Two days ago, surely she is dead by now."

After a while, while sadness called Martha into silence, Alice said, "Let's go tell her child".

Martha said with a smile, "Everyone will be notified soon. See? She did not die of aging!"

Alice, "Yes, but it is more like suicide."

Martha, "She was eighty-two years old, not eighteen! There is no reason for an old person to commit suicide while she is at the brink of death. She only chose her own type of death."

Alice, "People will definitely say that aging had messed up her mind, so she went to the desert and died."

Martha, "She knew well that she had not lost her mind and went to the desert willingly. She died due to the fatigue of desert trekking! She did not die of aging! Let me assure you. I want to go to the desert too and I do not want to die of aging."

She said the last sentence softly while avoiding looking at her friends. She was not sure what she was saying and was afraid that no one would accompany her. After a brief pause, she added, "Do you agree to go to the Atacama together?"

Marcela smiled bitterly, "We are still alive, but aging has buried our emotions so deeply that it seems they had not existed from the start. Believe me, I still like to laugh loudly, cry, flirt, think about success, and dance. But aging, this terrible mask! It choked all my emotions one by one. No! I do not let it put its hand on me and kill me."

Then she addressed the whole assembly, "We have to defeat it before it is too late."

Martha, "What did Marcela say?"

Alice replied, "She comes to the desert with you!" she looked at her friends and added, "I will go too!"

The triplets also decided to accompany Martha.

As a result, according to the date designated at Martha's home, the friends gathered near the Atacama two days later at midnight to *defeat aging*, as Marcela had put it. However, it was scheduled that they go to the Atacama the day after the meeting, but Alice remarked that one day was too short a time to say goodbye to children, grandchildren, and great-grandchildren. She had eleven children, thirty-nine grandchildren, and eight great-grandchildren. According to the draw, the result of which was already determined, she spent the last night at her last child's home and joined her friends thereafter.

Martha, Marcella, and Alice, after they had been waiting long enough for the triplet sisters and found out they would not come, started out.

Alice asked, "Did Isabel go to the Atacama from here as well?"

Martha, "I do not know. Maybe. Look, I have brought some water and fruits. What have *you* brought?"

Marcela opened her bag and showed it to Martha. Martha looked at the small amount of food inside the bag and commented, "You have got a nice bag there!"

Alice, "I also brought two fried chickens, some chocolate and two bottles of water."

Marcela, "Do you think we will die by starving or fatigue and heatstroke?"

Martha, "It does not matter. Anyhow, we will not die of old age, friends!"

Alice, "Any of us dies sooner; the other two will have to keep going regardless of her! I hope no one is tempted to return in the middle of the track."

Marta got Alice's hint and realized that she, like herself, doubted that Marcela could ever make it. So, to remind the scary face of old age to Marcella once more, she started to tell a memory, "A week ago, when I returned home from the graveyard, I gently fell down. People gathered to lift me up and did not allow me to get off the ground. They thought I could not manage it! I was already nearly throwing up by seeing their upset faces and their compassion for a white-haired person who has fallen, but their comments made me furious, 'Poor old woman! Indeed, old age is painful! The old woman lost her balance! The old woman's ankle twisted suddenly!'

"When I got up, I said that part of the ground was slippery, be careful, and that was why I fell down. One of them whispered to the person next to him, 'The elders are handicapped! Even if the ground is slippery, a youngster would never fall like that! Oh, old age....' ,do you believe this?!

"A moment later, a young man fell down at the same spot, way worse than me. They all laughed at him! He got up on his own and the continued on his path."

A Country Called the World

Incidentally, Marcela hated death more than them but since she was the oldest person among them, her friends thought perhaps she would return if she felt unable to go on.

Not long after they arrived at the Atacama, Marcela sensed a stabbing pain in her heart and suddenly hated herself deeply. She saw that aging had been settling in her heart for a long time and had possessed it and at that moment, it was laughing at her viciously. She had forgotten to bring her medication. If she died because of the severe pain that had attacked her heart, that death was due to aging because old age had weakened her heart. She stopped walking for a moment. When she saw her friends, who were at a little distance from her, stopped for her sake; fearing that lest she put her hand on the heart in front of them clenched her hands behind her and continued walking.

Martha asked her, "Are you tired?"

Marcela shook her head no. Alice massaged her shoulder with one hand and said jokingly, "whenever you get tired, tell me to take a break!"

Marcela, who could hardly breathe, laughed and said, "Time for a break is good when you have a definite destination. Not when we are going to walk to our death. Ha ha!"

Martha said, "In this situation, getting some rest means death itself! I wish all three of us to die together."

Marcela could not see anything for a moment. She felt the whiteness of the moonlight had clung to her eyes. Her hands were still clenched behind her back. She mumbled with a faint voice, "I think I got tired!"

Before she fell backward, Alice and Martha held her awkwardly and softly laid her on the ground. Martha held her left ear, which was not totally deaf yet in front of Marcella's nose. When she realized that she was dead, she unwrapped a large shawl she had worn around her waist and spread it on her face.

Alice whispered, "Hey, old age! See how this woman defeated you!"

Since Marcela walked very slowly, they were not far from their starting point unlike Isabel. After Marcela's death, they were so tired that they walked even slower than before, but fortunately, no one saw them and they continued to walk for a couple of hours after sunrise.

At a distance from them, there was a copper mine with two fairly tall watchtowers. Four disabled brothers – who were born with one arm that had grown only to the elbow – who could not work in the mine, were there round the clock. The mine did not need a watchtower, but since those four men were not in a good physical shape to work in the mine, and on the other hand, there was no job for them to support their subsistence, the kind mine contractor built two watchtowers for them so they deserve a salary for tolerating heat at daytime and the cold at night. One of the watchmen who was peeping into houses with his new binoculars, said excitedly, "Hey! I can see the tiniest creatures with these binoculars! And what strange things can be seen with these binoculars!"

Another one, who could not believe what he saw through the binoculars, asked, "Do you see them too? Do you see those two individuals in the desert?"

Martha and Alice were extremely fatigued and were on the brink of falling.

Alice said, "Do not you think it is strange that none of the triplets told our families where we are?"

Martha said sarcastically, "They certainly did not want to blow the hangout until some day they come here too!"

Alice said happily, "I feel I cannot walk anymore!"

Martha, "No, it is not the time yet! I still have energy!"

Alice said breathlessly, "How to die-hard are you, granny! We made it well! I do not want to look behind, but I know we have covered a lot of distance", and added, "I really feel I am dying."

Martha helped her to sit on the ground. She rested her head on her knee and held her hand in front of her face so at least the sunlight does not hurt her in the last moments of her life. Alice, who inhaled and exhaled with difficulty, said with tears in her eyes, "I am dying of fatigue! Of fatigue!"

Martha started to cry and fanned her face by her other hand and said, "No. Not now. Please hold on a little longer. Hold on a bit so that we die together. If you want, I will piggyback you the rest of the way."

Alice, "Do not forget to eat the food. I have brought a lot of foodstuffs!" and as her eyes were closing, she added, ". . . chocolate. . . water."

Martha was very scared. She consumed the little energy that was left for her to lift Alice's large torso. But she was unsuccessful, she felt dizzy and fell belly up beside Alice.

About an hour and twenty minutes later, when Martha regained her consciousness, she saw her children were looking at her. It did not take her too long to realize that she was in the hospital. Her eyes closed again. She heard her children's voices, but could not speak, and afterward, when she regained full consciousness, she decided not to speak because she was very upset about someone saving her life. She helplessly closed her eyes and remembered Alice.

She whispered under her breath, "Alice."

One of the children, after carefully watching her mouth that for the twentieth time was called 'Alice. . . Ali ...' said to her, "She is here, mother! Alice is at the side of your bed."

Martha slowly turned her head toward Alice. Alice was still unconscious. A while ago, her children, grandchildren, and great-grandchildren all had come to the hospital and since the order at the hospital was compromised and their presence filled the room, inevitably only her children stayed. However, there was still not free space in the small room where Alice and Martha were hospitalized to accommodate all of her eleven children. Therefore, they had to draw lots to choose three persons from among themselves to stay with the mother.

When Alice's children saw Marta came back to consciousness approached her and placed themselves among her four children.

One of them said, "Ms. Ruepke! Do you hear me?"

Martha did not answer, because she knew he was supposed to ask why she had gone to the Atacama. They hoped when Alice regained consciousness, there was nobody there to coordinate the answer with her. She found herself at grave danger and it was possible that she would be submitted to the custody of her children to the end of her life and they might assume that she was an old woman with a mental disorder. She had to find a good reason for going to the Atacama. What was worse was that they had survived and could no longer overcome death as a result of aging.

 Half an hour later, the two watchmen who had taken Alice and Martha to the hospital, found Marcella's corpse. By hearing the sound of the weeping of Marcella's children, Alice and Martha's children felt twice as much thankful as they were before because their mothers were still alive, and when the doctor told them, 'A miracle! Surely if a young person covered half of that distance he would be wasted or at least caught an incurable disease....', they were both more afraid of their mothers and also loved them much more than before.

Outside the hospital, Isabel's only daughter with her husband stopped the two watchmen and said, "Please, look again. Search further and find my mother too."

The watchmen, happy and cheerful of what they had done recently, made a face like doctors and promised her to do their best to find her mother. But when they patrolled the whole area with the car and searched from the top of the watchtower, they did not found any trace of the old woman they have been told about by Isabel's daughter.

Marta pretended that she was asleep and the doctor said it would be better than she rested there for a while, and also told Alice's children not to crowd around their mother. Sometimes later, nobody was in their room. Alice noticed from the corner of her eyes that Martha was looking at her, calling her with a murmuring voice. When she made sure their children had left and they would be alone for a while, she said with a calm and sick tone, "I wish at least we had caught some incurable or deadly disease from the Atacama."

Martha raised her head slightly and said, "Were you conscious?!"

Alice, "Oh, aging, aging, aging. . ."

Martha, "Forget aging! What should we tell the kids?"

Alice, "I do not know. Did they find Marcela?"

Martha, "Yes. The vultures had not noticed her yet," and she asked again sadly, "What should we tell the kids?"

Alice joked, "We will say we went desert trekking!"

Marta said, "And Marcela died during desert trekking?!"

Suddenly she pulled herself up on her elbow and said anxiously, "Marcela died! Isabel too! If they were alive, we could say that we launched a desert trekking contest and went desert trekking and another kind of childish excuses. What will the kids think of us?! They will say aging has spoiled our minds!"

Alice did not say anything and stared at Martha without moving a finger. Martha realized that she was talking too loud and glanced at the door lest if someone arrived, she pretends to be asleep promptly.

She looked at Alice again and said, "Alice? Did you understand what I said? Alice! Alice! my God!"

When Marta was scared enough, Alice said while still looking at her, "We have no choice. In any case, they will say we have lost our minds."

Martha took a deep breath and said; "I thought you are dead!" then she put her hand on her forehead and closed her eyes to surrender to the future.

A Country Called the World

Alice and Martha spent the rest of their lives with their children like before. The psychiatrist warned their children to pay more attention to them and respect and love them more to prevent any such similar events or even worse.

Just at the moment she lit up the lantern, her grandmother arrived. At least conversation with the grandmother distracted her from paranoid thoughts. When she pondered a little bit, she thought it might be better to tell the grandmother about the incident, so perhaps they could come up with a solution to the ordeal she was going through. But on the other hand, she knew that if two or three days passed and the cops did not show up, everything would be fine and go back to normal. Anyway, she was suspiciously silent, and it was necessary to say something and chat with the grandmother as in the recent nights and mock people.

To hide the anxiety and blunder, while she knew the grandmother's reply, asked sheepishly, "How can you walk around without the light?"

The grandmother put her shopping bag, which contained a piece of meat, ten eggs, a medium-sized pot full of milk, and two blocks of cheese, at a corner and muttered repeatedly under her breath, "Who has got the money! Money!"

She had been muttering that sentence incessantly since she left the house of the last customer a couple of minutes ago until she reached her home.

She picked up the bag again, looked at Saleh, and said, "No, you do not walk this corner. But anyway, it is not bad to take your absent-mindedness seriously. I will be right back." She went to the kitchen in the dark, put the bag there, and returned.

A Country Called the World

She started to take off her socks and said loudly, "*Agadiris* are penniless, do you believe it?! We have regressed a thousand years! The exchange of goods with goods."

Saleh laughed and said, "Exchange of the future forecast with the goods!"

The grandmother said, "Anyway, it is a commodity too. Especially this last customer! One of his camels has disappeared. He asked me to find the thief."

Saleh, "Did you find the thief?"

Grandmother, "Yes. It was the easiest thing I did today," then she crawled toward the lantern on all fours to closely inspect Saleh's face.

Saleh, "Did you darken the tattoos?"

The grandmother used her index finger to touch, first, the sun between the eyebrows, and then, the three small circles that she had already tattooed on her chin, and said, "They look as such? Maybe it is because of the lantern's light. I have come close to look into your eyes," she looked more thoroughly at Saleh's eyes and added, "There is a bad future ahead of you! A future not so far off. Perhaps tomorrow. What have you done?"

Saleh looked at the grandmother desperately.

The grandmother said, "Look here."

Saleh looked at the shadow of the grandmother's hand on the wall. The shadow took the shape of a baby and the grandmother cried out like a baby. Then, the shadow was that of a four-year-old child who was weeping due to getting lost at the marketplace. Then it was a thirteen-year-old teenager who was upset because of his wrongdoing, then a young man who sang at the corner of a prison cell, a middle-aged man who was still imprisoned, and an old man who with clenched hands behind him, climbed the uphill path to his home.

Saleh said grudgingly, "What an ill fate is waiting me."

The grandmother said, "Spill it out. There's always a way to change the future."

A horse rider was passing slowly in front of the village houses, looking at his left and right. He felt mildly uncomfortable to see that the long alleys of the village do not cross, but that discomfort was nothing compared to the incident that annoyed him in the evening. After a while, he found the alley he was looking for. He tied the horse to a corner and entered the only alley with stairs to reach the desired house. The young man looked closely at the iron doors. The names of the landlords were written on all of the doors. The young man reached the middle of the alley and held the lantern up in front of the door of a house and moved closer to see better. Only the letters *S* and *G* were faintly visible on the door and the rest of the letters were erased. The young man smiled bitterly and said, "Grandmother and Saleh!"

Saleh sobbed, "I and some of my friends, that is, six of my friends, went to the drapery shop owned by the uncle of one of my classmates, Taher, who is the only nerdy student in the class. His uncle is not too old, but a little deaf. We were supposed to steal six fist-sized money bags from the pot wherein he stored his coins. Taher distracted his uncle by asking him to talk about the memories of his youth! What he always does anyway. He used to repeatedly advise us, without there being any misconduct on our part, and talked about the time he was our age. When Taher succeeded in distracting him, I entered my shop. I carried the six bags one at a time inside my overcoat and took them to the back of the shop where my friends were standing and everyone got his share. Taher was supposed to join us when we went away from the shop. But as soon as he interrupted his uncle's speech and said, 'I have to go, tell me the rest of it later,' his uncle laughed and said, 'Bad friends will ruin you,' and while Taher was running away from him, his uncle added, 'I will call the cops tonight.'

When we went far enough from the shop, I realized that I had mistakenly stolen six bags instead of seven. But Taher was not upset about the fact that he did not get any coins, and from the time he joined us, he sat at a corner, swang his legs worriedly and did not talk. Indifferent to him, we were busy talking and laughing about what we wanted to do with our money, when one of my friends said to Taher, 'Do not be afraid, it is over.' But Taher was shaking with fear and repeatedly mumbled word. All of us became silent, and I asked, 'What did you say?' Taher said, 'The cops, the cops,' then he looked at us and said, 'He noticed you and said that he was going to call the cops.' Since we forced him to cooperate and he was always afraid of us, so we considered the possibility that he had sold us out."

Someone knocked on the door.

Saleh freaked out and said, "Forgive me, grandma. I am sorry."

The grandmother opened the door regardless of Saleh's weeping.

The young man said, "Do you mind I come in? I am not a cop. I am Taher's brother."

Saleh's anxiety was exacerbated from the moment he heard the knock on the door, he was stuck between running to the kitchen and running to the cellar. But he stopped when he looked out of the window and saw the cops were not there. The young man entered the house along with the grandmother. Saleh recognized him.

The young man said, "So you threatened him to tell his family that he had masterminded the plan and you just carried it out."

Saleh's lips moved again and he looked at his grandmother.

The grandmother said, "Do not cry. He is not going to hurt you."

The young man said, "I did not call the cops, you can keep the coins, just answer my question. You are your friends' gang leader and if you do not answer my question correctly, I will have to call the cops and then I'll go after your friends. Or not! Perhaps having you arrested should suffice."

Saleh fell at the man's feet and said, "I am sorry."

The grandmother lifted him up and seated him right at the place where he sat before the arrival of the Taher's brother and sat down next to him. The young man, who thought it might be impolite to remain standing, also sat down.

Young man, "Is Taher scared of your bullying, or you keep tabs on him that you scare him by his weak points?"

Saleh, "He was afraid of us in the past, but later, when he got used to our beatings, we found his point of weakness and. . ."

The young man said, "I see," he stroked his long beard and smiled with satisfaction and taught to himself, "He is tough! He is not afraid of battery. Everyone has a weakness and fears its disclosure. My brother is not a coward or a weak person!"

A Country Called the World

After a while, when Saleh stopped sobbing, the young started to leave the house. After he reassured the grandmother that they had not called the police, he said goodbye to her and left the house. The grandmother hugged Saleh and Saleh continued to weep more copiously than before.

A Country Called the World

A Country Called the World

Morocco

The Point of Weakness

Just at the moment, she lit up the lantern, her grandmother arrived. At least conversation with the grandmother distracted her from paranoid thoughts. When she pondered a little bit, she thought it might be better to tell the grandmother about the incident, so perhaps they could come up with a solution to the ordeal she was going through. But on the other hand, she knew that if two or three days passed and the cops did not show up, everything would be fine and go back to normal. Anyway, she was suspiciously silent, and it was necessary to say something and chat with the grandmother as in the recent nights and mock people.

To hide the anxiety and blunder, while she knew the grandmother's reply, asked sheepishly, "How can you walk around without the light?"

The grandmother put her shopping bag, which contained a piece of meat, ten eggs, a medium-sized pot full of milk, and two blocks of cheese, at a corner and muttered repeatedly under her breath, "Who has got the money! Money!"

She had been muttering that sentence incessantly since she left the house of the last customer a couple of minutes ago until she reached her home.

She picked up the bag again, looked at Saleh, and said, "No, you do not walk this corner. But anyway, it is not bad to take your absent-mindedness seriously. I will be right back." She went to the kitchen in the dark, put the bag there, and returned.

She started to take off her socks and said loudly, "*Agadiris* are penniless, do you believe it?! We have regressed a thousand years! The exchange of goods with goods."

Saleh laughed and said, "Exchange of the future forecast with the goods!"

The grandmother said, "Anyway, it is a commodity too. Especially this last customer! One of his camels has disappeared. He asked me to find the thief."

Saleh, "Did you find the thief?"

Grandmother, "Yes. It was the easiest thing I did today," then she crawled toward the lantern on all fours to closely inspect Saleh's face.

Saleh, "Did you darken the tattoos?"

The grandmother used her index finger to touch, first, the sun between the eyebrows, and then, the three small circles that she had already tattooed on her chin, and said, "They look as such? Maybe it is because of the lantern's light. I have come close to look into your eyes," she looked more thoroughly at Saleh's eyes and added, "There is a bad future ahead of you! A future not so far off. Perhaps tomorrow. What have you done?"

Saleh looked at the grandmother desperately.

The grandmother said, "Look here."

Saleh looked at the shadow of the grandmother's hand on the wall. The shadow took the shape of a baby and the grandmother cried out like a baby. Then, the shadow was that of a four-year-old child who was weeping due to getting lost at the marketplace. Then it was a thirteen-year-old teenager who was upset because of his wrongdoing, then a young man who sang at the corner of a prison cell, a middle-aged man who was still imprisoned, and an old man who with clenched hands behind him, climbed the uphill path to his home.

Saleh said grudgingly, "What an ill fate is waiting for me."

The grandmother said, "Spill it out. There's always a way to change the future."

A horse rider was passing slowly in front of the village houses, looking at his left and right. He felt mildly uncomfortable to see that the long alleys of the village do not cross, but that discomfort was nothing compared to the incident that annoyed him in the evening. After a while, he found the alley he was looking for. He tied the horse to a corner and entered the only alley with stairs to reach the desired house. The young man looked closely at the iron doors. The names of the landlords were written on all of the doors. The young man reached the middle of the alley and held the lantern up in front of the door of a house and moved closer to see better. Only the letters *S* and *G* were faintly visible on the door and the rest of the letters were erased. The young man smiled bitterly and said, "Grandmother and Saleh!"

Saleh sobbed, "I and some of my friends, that is, six of my friends, went to the drapery shop owned by the uncle of one of my classmates, Taher, who is the only nerdy student in the class. His uncle is not too old, but a little deaf. We were supposed to steal six fist-sized money bags from the pot wherein he stored his coins. Taher distracted his uncle by asking him to talk about the memories of his youth! What he always does anyway. He used to repeatedly advise us, without there being any misconduct on our part and talked about the time he was our age. When Taher succeeded in distracting him, I entered my shop. I carried the six bags one at a time inside my overcoat and took them to the back of the shop where my friends were standing and everyone got his share. Taher was supposed to join us when we went away from the shop. But as soon as he interrupted his uncle's speech and said, 'I have to go, tell me the rest of it later,' his uncle laughed and said, 'Bad friends will ruin you,' and while Taher was running away from him, his uncle added, 'I will call the cops tonight.'

When we went far enough from the shop, I realized that I had mistakenly stolen six bags instead of seven. But Taher was not upset about the fact that he did not get any coins, and from the time he joined us, he sat at a corner, swang his legs worriedly and did not talk. Indifferent to him, we were busy talking and laughing about what we wanted to do with our money, when one of my friends said to Taher, 'Do not be afraid, it is over.' But Taher was shaking with fear and repeatedly mumbled a word. All of us became silent, and I asked, 'What did you say?' Taher said, 'The cops, the cops,' then he looked at us and said, 'He noticed you and said that he was going to call the cops.' Since we forced him to cooperate and he was always afraid of us, so we considered the possibility that he had sold us out."

Someone knocked on the door.

Saleh freaked out and said, "Forgive me, grandma. I am sorry."

The grandmother opened the door regardless of Saleh's weeping.

The young man said, "Do you mind I come in? I am not a cop. I am Taher's brother."

A Country Called the World

Saleh's anxiety was exacerbated from the moment he heard the knock on the door, he was stuck between running to the kitchen and running to the cellar. But he stopped when he looked out of the window and saw the cops were not there. The young man entered the house along with the grandmother. Saleh recognized him.

The young man said, "So you threatened him to tell his family that he had masterminded the plan and you just carried it out."

Saleh's lips moved again and he looked at his grandmother.

The grandmother said, "Do not cry. He is not going to hurt you."

The young man said, "I did not call the cops, you can keep the coins, just answer my question. You are your friends' gang leader and if you do not answer my question correctly, I will have to call the cops and then I'll go after your friends. Or not! Perhaps having you arrested should suffice."

Saleh fell at the man's feet and said, "I am sorry."

The grandmother lifted him up and seated him right at the place where he sat before the arrival of the Taher's brother and sat down next to him. The young man, who thought it might be impolite to remain to stand, also sat down.

Young man, "Is Taher scared of your bullying, or you keep tabs on him that you scare him by his weak points?"

Saleh, "He was afraid of us in the past, but later, when he got used to our beatings, we found his point of weakness and. . ."

The young man said, "I see," he stroked his long beard and smiled with satisfaction and taught to himself, "He is tough! He is not afraid of the battery. Everyone has a weakness and fears its disclosure. My brother is not a coward or a weak person!"

After a while, when Saleh stopped sobbing, the young started to leave the house. After he reassured the grandmother that they had not called the police, he said goodbye to her and left the house. The grandmother hugged Saleh and Saleh continued to weep more copiously than before.

A Country Called the World

Russia

To Fly with the Feathers in the Pillow

One of the most important reasons for the popularity of *The Seagull*[3] play in the Moscow Art Theater was Marina Tarkovsky's role as Nina[4], which made her famous overnight. At the end of the third act when Trigorin[5] and Nina was snogging, the male audience looked with envy at the young man who starred in the role of Trigorin, and some, just to experience the fleeting moment of the kissing scene, stopped Stanislavsky[6] whenever they saw him and begged him to grant them an audition appointment and test them for the Trigorin's role. At the end of the same play, when Marina in the role of Nina began to sob, the noise of the weeping audience filled the hall and the actors had to perform louder, and when Treplev[7] said to Nina, "I was cursing you, I hated you . . . But at all times, I knew my soul forever belongs to you. I kiss the dirt on which you walked . . ." many spectators fainted.

Ms. Marina Tarkovsky was a beautiful muscovite lady who had the rare opportunity to shine like a star in the theater without being abused. Every time someone, especially a journalist,

---

[3] A plays by Chekhov.
[4] A character in The Seagull play (Nina Mikhailovna Zarechnaya).
[5] A character in The Seagull play (Boris Alexeyevich Trigorin).
[6] Director of The Seagull play at the Moscow Art Theater. Konstantin Sergey Stanislavsky was one of the most important actors and directors of the Russian theatre, a founder of the Moscow Art Theater.
[7] A character in The Seagull play (Konstantin Gavrilovich Treplev).

asked how she had climbed the ladder of success, she answered with just one sentence.

She used to bite her lip and say, "It was hard. Really hard," and anxiously looked at the Inquirer for a few moments with her blue eyes.

It was unusual that someone asked her questions unrelated to her personal interest in the theater, her future in the career, or other common questions. If another question was asked, the purpose of asking it was to proceed to a frequent question to ultimately reach the answer that the people would have liked to hear, "How many years have you been performing in the theater? How did you discover your talent? What is your advice for those who want to enter this career? Are there any risks threatening them in the process of becoming an actress? What problems have you faced to become an actress?"

Apparently, people just could not believe that she could have become a star without being subject to extortion. So, they mostly asked her about her path to success, so maybe Marina would let the cat out of the bag and say, for example, "I have been frequently abused sexually in the course of my career."

That was a topic of interest to many people in Moscow, and when they came together and talked about Marina, they chatted about the impossibility of her not being abused, and circulated rumors about her.

A Country Called the World

- "She has an affair with Stanislavsky! She is Chekhov's[8] nephew! She is an aristocrat and paved her way into show business with money and collusion!"

Anytime Marina was the target of multiple questions with repetitive inquiries, she struggled to overcome her wrath and kept cool in the presence of the person but afterward, she was upset and asked herself how a human being could be so mean.

When Marina figured out what was her real purpose in life, and with that reckoning could overcome her ignorance and to seize the booty of self-knowledge from it, she had indeed become a privileged person who made people jealous. One of the great qualities that put her apart from both the professions and also all of the people of Moscow was her gut feeling that the time flies so fast. Therefore, to get the best of it, it was better to continue what she was already doing; during the day when she was busy practicing, every couple of hours, she reminded herself what day of the week and date of the month it was.

A January night, when Marina was returning from the show, a middle-aged man jumped in front of her coach. The coachman nearly missed the man by a hair. The middle-aged man took out a pen and a paper from his loose-fitting overcoat that tended to slip off his body, and handed them to Marina, asking for her signature. Marina had not quite finished the signature when the man grasped the coach door and said, "Please let me talk to you! I promise not to say anything that would disturb you. I must talk to you!"

---

[8] Anton Pavlovich Chekhov (۱۸۶۰ -۱۹۰۴) was a Russian playwright and short-story writer, who is considered to be among the greatest writers of short fiction in history.

A Country Called the World

Marina looked at the man's hands that had membranes like duck's claw and were placed on the red velvet inner cushion of the coach door, and then stuck out her head and looked around. The street was empty but the man's voice and his childish jumping up and down could attract too much attention. She looked back at the man again. She felt pity for his commoner and disturbed looks and did not want to kill the guy's enthusiasm, "Get on. But I do not have much time to talk. I will reach home in a few minutes."

The man, amazed and glad to have Marina at arm's length, climbed into the coach and the coachman started out. The man had a strange and unreasonable feeling that he would run short of time no matter how fast he could talk and communicate his intention.

Therefore, he started to talk immediately after he seated himself, "I am from Sergiyev Posad. My daughter, Vita, loves theater. It is spectacular when she mimics you! She is only fourteen and my wife and I would like her to be an actress too. But . . . you know how climbing the ladder of success is risky and difficult for a girl, especially in the show business. Do you mind if I send her to you for training? I will send her expenses to you every month."

Marina suspected for a moment that the man would certainly want to peek into her life via her daughter, which of course, was not uncommon for the people to do so, but then she realized that his appearance looked more businesslike than someone who would waste time for such futile attempts. Moreover, there was a kind of honesty and naivety in his eyes. Although Marina had not trained anyone up to that time or taught in an actors' training center, it was the dude's lucky day, and at that moment she decided to give it a shot once and for all.

- "No problem. But nobody should know that I teach your daughter. Because in that case, many people will rush to me. I hate teaching."

The man happily swore to all that was sacred to him not to tell anyone, and in a span of fewer than five minutes from the time that he had gotten on the coach, he succeeded to lure Marina into giving away her address. He got down and told Marina that he would send her daughter to her house within two days.

Marina asked, "How do you know that I will be a good teacher for your daughter?"

"I just want her to walk along the same path that you did," replied the man.

"The day after tomorrow at 10 AM, your daughter must be in my house, then;" said Marina with a smile.

Two days later, at noon, Marina's housekeeper was cleaning the stairs when she saw a girl playing with a stray cat. The girl had forgotten that she had to report to Marina. However, a bit later, she went to her house after cuddling the cat. The maid was busy working with her back to the yard gate, but she sensed the girl's presence and said, "Why are you crying? You had an appointment with the madam?"

The little girl stepped forward with eyes full of tears and said, "Yes. Excuse me, would you please give me a bowl of milk. I found this kitten right near the house."

The housekeeper was very sensitive to cats since they freaked her out. She wiped her hands with her checkered apron, returned slowly, and with a nearly screaming voice, said, "Stop there and do not get closer!"

Then she picked up the mop and the water bucket and immediately retreated into the house.

The maid met Marina in the corridor and said, "She is here! Crazy lass!"

"Is she in the yard?" asked Marina.

"Yes. I am going to fetch some milk for her kitty," replied the maid.

Marina tied her golden hair behind her head and went to the yard.

"Hi, Mr. Tarkovsky! I am Vita. Vita Shilovsky," the girl said, upon seeing her.

Marina went forward and after caressing her kitten, asked, "Why are you crying?"

The girl, with a tone like someone grieving for the loss of a beloved one, said, "Can you stand to hear what I am going to tell you?" and continued without waiting for Marina's reply, "When I got near your home, I saw two bellies up with a little distance apart, and this kitten was sucking milk from one of them. I thought they were asleep, but when I went closer, I saw both of them were dead. They were the parents of this kitten and presumably not a long time had passed since their death. This kitten is very hungry."

Marina called the maid, but she answered, "I do not come out," and she put the cup of milk at the door and retreated into the house.

A Country Called the World

Marina brought the cup of milk and the poor cat, upon seeing the milk, stretched its paws toward it. The cat was in Vita's hands and the cup of milk was in Marina's hands, and the cat was softly laid down while still lapping the milk.

"Our appointment was scheduled at ten, why are you late?" asked Marina.

Vita wiped her tears and replied, "I am sorry. I saw a flock of sheep on my way! Beautiful sheep! I asked the shepherd to fetch me one of the lambs to cuddle it. By the way, do you keep pets here?"

Marina, who a few moments ago, by seeing Vita's innocent face, braided Hannah hair, green eyes, and her neat and simple dress had reckoned that she could be a good actor, totally changed her mind; especially when she saw Vita held up her skirt and chased the chickens and ducks at the back of the yard.

A few days passed from Vita's arrival at Marina's house, but she did not show any interest in theater. Instead of practicing, she spent her days from dawn to dusk among chickens and ducks and other animals owned by one of Marina's neighbors. Marina, in spite of realizing the disinterest of Vita in the show business, did not say anything and did not notify the girl's father either. Vita reminded Marina of her own youth, the time when she, with great courage and confidence, did not allow anyone distracts her from what she was interested in.

On a cloudy day, when Marina had her breakfast earlier than others and was working at the corner of the house on the play she had written by herself, she looked at Vita, who had just had woken up and was sitting at the table, and said, "Ok! Today is Wednesday, February 5. After you finished your breakfast, we will read a play together and start learning the basics of the theater," and winked at the maid.

Vita was prepared to endure any ordeal to stay at Marina's house, and thus replied, "Oh yeah! That is great!"

Marina laughed, "You crazy bitch!" and then added, "You should become a veterinarian!"

Suddenly, Vita jumped out of her seat as if bitten by something, ran to Marina, grasped her hands and said, "Dear madam! If my father sends mail, please tell him I am practicing every day and I am actually a phenomenal actress. Tell him I will certainly become a successful actress."

Gradually, tears gathered in Vita's eyes. Marina took her shoulders and said with a serious voice, "If you love animals and you want to be a veterinarian, then try to get what you want. Do not waste your time here."

Vita cried, "I tried my best to come here, far from my parent's prying eyes, so at least I could spend my time with the animals for a while. They absolutely abhor animals and they do not let me become a vet. They even do not allow me to touch an animal. About two months ago, when you became a star and your reputation spread around, my father was very keen to bring me to Moscow to see your performance. Finally, last month I came with him and saw your performance. From the very next day, I mimicked you all the time. It did not take long for my parents to believe that I love acting. Apparently, I came here to do theater, but in my heart, I just think about animals. About treatment and maintenance of sick animals, keeping hundreds of sheep and cows and . . ." Vita began to sob.

A Country Called the World

The housekeeper, while she was cleaning up the breakfast table, said under her breath, "Like a captive thrown into the depths of an unfathomable waterless well, I do not know where I am and what is waiting for me."[9]

Marina, with Vita in her arms, thought to herself how much Vita was similar to her. As much as it seemed unlikely that Marina would someday become an actor, it was equally unlikely that Vita would become a vet.

At night, when Marina narrated the story of her life to Vita and told her what a bumpy journey she had gone through, Vita felt a strong sense of courage and bravery. At that night, when Vita went to bed, she hugged her pillow tight and slept.

– "It was very unlikely for me to be an actor. It was so doubtful as if someone decides to fly with the feathers in the pillow. I did it! I flew with the feathers in my pillow!"

---

[9] Quoted from The Seagull play.

A Country Called the World

Finland

Incompetent or Tolerant

It was the second night in a row that the young sheriff, through the window of his office, saw a person approached the police station gate and then returned without entering. After making sure that the guy was the same old Erkie Jacobsen, the bookworm and his elementary school friend, a few nights later, when he bumped into him in the town and greeted him, he decided to invite him home for dinner.

"Same glasses, same hair!" he nudged Erki's arm and said jokingly, "But this is not the same book!"

Erki smoothed his shiny flat hair, which was combed delicately to the right, and showed the book to the sheriff, "Since those times, at least a thousand books have passed through my hands."

The sheriff glanced at the book and said, "The Last Day of a Condemned Man![1] Good taste. Do you still live in Joensuu?"

"No, I have relocated here just last month," replied Erki, then he looked at the star on the sheriff's shirt and said with a smile, "So, you are now a policeman!"

The sheriff laughed a self-congratulatory laugh and nodded. A moment later, he said with a friendly tone, "Well, my friend! I have to go. Will I be honored to be your host tonight for dinner?"

---

[1] A novel by Victor Hugo. 0

A Country Called the World

Although Erki had to prepare the layouts of a lot of books and did not feel any intimacy with the sheriff, he needed to talk about an important subject that had occupied his mind with someone at the level of the sheriff. Therefore, he accepted his invitation which he considered as good luck, and said, "Of course, the honor is mine."

The sheriff gave him his home address, and they agreed that Erkie would be there at 8 PM.

On that day, when they said goodbye and departed a few steps away from each other, Erki turned his head, looked at him, and said, "Indeed, this uniform really fits you well!"

The sheriff, with a serious face, pumped up his chest and lowered the pitch of his voice and said, "Thanks!" then he returned to his normal manners and laughed, "It seems that you have been born like that from the beginning, too!"

The weather had become sunny after a long time and it was no longer possible to look at the snow. Therefore, Erkie, on the poaching of his house and with narrowed eyes, stared at the snow that had reached the knees and made the snow shovel an integral part of the people's everyday life. Singing of children in the school bus, laughter of the young couple who were building a snowman, cawing of crows, and the sound of the snow shovel of the old man next door who was impatiently shoveling the snow off his roof; none could disrupt the Erki's line of thoughts. He was thinking of his own and the sheriff's childhood. Even in those days, the sheriff was a strong bully. So much that when his friends fought with someone, they asked him for help and nobody could really beat the sheriff. Since his youth, his bullying had become charismatic in a way that no attire other than a police uniform could complement it.

However, Erki was very weak and disadvantaged. He could not defend himself. The sheriff was right. He was born like that from the beginning and the matter that had recently made him hate his brother was nothing new.

When his brother got out of the house and climbed into his car, Erki poured his half-finished coffee in the yard and went inside. His brother, who had been ferociously abusive toward him and pulled a self-righteous face until a few days ago, glanced for a moment at the house door in the side mirror and then started to go with discomfort. He thought that he had paid for what he had done and Erki had forgiven him, but that was not the case.

At night, Erki put on his bear fur coat that he had purchased with his savings of many months, so if the sheriff liked the coat, he could brag that he himself had hunted the bear. He examined himself in the mirror and decided to press his teeth tightly together at the times that he will not be talking because he thought his face would look more attractive that way.

A few minutes later, he stood in front of sheriff house's door with black boots, gloves and woolen hat, and brown overcoat and trousers and knocked after a brief pause, 'Just in time!'

Erki was anxious to see the sheriff's family members. Before he seated himself at the table opposite to his friend, he awkwardly took off his coat and while hanging it on the hanger, noticed a deer head wall mount pinned to the wall above the fireplace and then saw the fox fur skin floor rug in front of the fireplace and felt pity. He hoped that the material of his expensive coat was not for real.

The sheriff introduced his family members and began to eat. The sheriff's wife noticed Erki's worried eyes and to make him feel at home, smiled and said, "My husband told me you are shy! And we made a bet that whether you would come for dinner!"

Erki laughed, and in a way that mostly conveyed rudeness rather than self-confidence, asked, "Who won?"

Ms. Lonrot glanced at her husband.

The family's little girl said immediately, "Dad always wins!"

The sheriff triumphantly thumped his chest a couple of times and winked at Erki, who was looking at him with a smile.

After dinner, Erki and the sheriff sat beside the fireplace and Ms. Lonrot went upstairs with her three children to tell them a story.

Sheriff, "Do not you smoke?"

Erkie shook his head. He had already laughed a lot while the sheriff told him his memories and was eager to talk to the sheriff about his problem. Therefore, as soon as he found the opportunity, he gazed at the fire so the sheriff would think his mind is elsewhere and ask him about it.

However, the sheriff was twice as curious than the day he saw him in front of the police headquarters, not because of Erki's fire-gazing but because of the muscles on both sides of his jaw which contracted every few seconds. He thought the problem must have been critical to making a person as calm as Erkie so nervous. The sheriff himself had experienced such a mood which was a sign of his nervousness. So, he asked, "By the way, was it you who approached the police station a few days ago but did not come in?"

"Yes, yes!" confirmed Erki and added, "Something happened that I will tell you."

A Country Called the World

He thought to himself how lucky he was that he could spill his heart to a man of law in a spacious and happy house. A few days ago, he was at the edge of disclosing the problem to one of his friends who was always sad and depressed. Erki knew that his sad friend could not argue with him and would be easily defeated.

The sheriff, to convince Erki that he could comfortably tell him his problem, articulated his words, "I saw you twice! Twice in front of the police headquarters. You approached and returned. If there is any problem, tell me, my friend."

Erkie, "I and my brother bought a house in the partnership that needs repairs and at present, only one of its rooms can be used. One day, that is, just six days ago, my brother brought her girlfriend home and pulled me to a corner and told me to go outside for half an hour. Although I did not want to go and I was busy, but I went out to avoid violating his emotions and instincts. It was 9 PM and I was supposed to return home at nine thirty. Since I had not yet received my salary and had no money to go to a coffee shop or a warm spot, I walked for half an hour. Half an hour later, I returned home, freezing. They were still there. Again, I walked the streets and the parks, and every half an hour when I went back, they were still home. They left home after three hours. At midnight, when my brother returned home, I told him quite logically and seriously that his behavior was not right at all, because it made me kill my time. Something I hate so much. He did not take me seriously and acquitted himself by laughing it away. The next night, he again urged me to go out of the house. Again, I did not say anything and told him I would be back in half an hour.

He barked back, "If you see the car is still in front of the house, do not enter the house, please."

Upon hearing that, I got so angry that I had the motivation to beat the hell out of him. But I thought to myself there must be a better way too. That time, I was walking outside for about four hours. The cold penetrated my body. My head was aching badly and I thought that my headache and teeth chattering were mostly due to the nervousness rather than the cold weather. When I got home, I cursed him and I slept. With blatant cheekiness, he asked me to go out of the house the next night too. This time I stood against his request but he kicked me out. I threatened him to sue him . . ."

The Sheriff could not help not to interrupt Erkie, and asked, "Why did not you file a complaint?! Why did not you take action?!"

Erki, with his head and hand gestures called him to keep calm, and to go on and state the reason, "The last time I went out of the house, I got mad. I wanted to damage his car or kick my way in and beat him, I wanted to take the police home, and though I could not prove my case that he had thrown me out of the house, it was enough just to defend myself as such and scare him. However, I regretted it every time. When I returned home about four hours later, I was not feeling well at all. In the early morning, I began to shake badly. He noticed my delirium and bad conditions and really freaked out. He knew I was very sensitive to the cold . . . (he rubbed his hands together and looked at the fireplace.) Ha, ha, cold intolerant! Indeed, four hours of cold can even knock down an elephant! Yes. He, who used to not to take my cold intolerance seriously, suffered moral remorse by seeing my ruin, took me to the car and drove me to the hospital. I stayed in the hospital for two days until I got well."

The sheriff asked with a confused look, "Did not you show any reaction?"

Erkie, "What would you have done if you were in my shoes?"

Sheriff, "Injustice! You are oppressed! If I was you, I would put him in his place."

Erkie leaned on the chair and, with the fineness of someone who has learned an important text by heart, said, "If I complained against him and at best, I could prove my case, he would be jailed for a short time. In that case, he would be called a criminal. Criminal! In the prison, we call both a murderer and a misdemeanor convict a criminal. Thus, I refused to complain because his future, and most importantly, our brotherhood, would have been ruined, which of course, has already been somewhat ruined. The next point is that, given my mental disorder, if I wanted to punish him physically, I would definitely have incurred serious injury to him or it would end in manslaughter. Since I knew I was weaker than him, I was going to attack him with a snow shovel. Well! Is it reasonable to imprison or kill someone who just wants to have some intimate moments with his girlfriend?"

It reminded the sheriff of plaintiffs who had suffered severe damages due to petty causes. But that case did not seem so simple to him. Therefore, He said, "He does not deserve to be dealt with because he wanted to be alone with his girlfriend, but he must be dealt with because he has oppressed you."

Erki, "He caused me to catch a cold and forced me to waste my time. But if I wanted to deal with him, he would either be imprisoned or suffered huge damage. It was not fair. Can you come up with a better idea than what I did? If I resisted, I had to file a petition or engage with him physically, either way."

The sheriff affirmed his opinion courteously, "And he is your brother."

Erkie, "Yes. However, I am not on speaking terms with him and it is unlikely that our relationship ever goes back to normal."

He thought that even if he had dealt with his brother, the avoidance to speak to each other would happen anyway. Therefore, the fact that he did not show any reaction gave him peace of mind, that is, while he would possibly never talk to his brother, but that incident could have a terrible ending, which it had not.

The sheriff thought intensively for a few moments to convince Erkie that he had to strongly react to his brother's behavior, and his forgiveness was nothing but acceptance of his oppression and incompetence. During the time Erkie was presenting his reasons for not to confront his brother, the sheriff was imagining himself in his shoes, hitting his brother's head hard to the car hood, kicking his way into the house, and humiliating him in front of his girlfriend, and so on and so forth.

All of a sudden, the sheriff felt great joy all over his body and soul as if he was on the verge of a great discovery, and asked, "What would you have done if you were not ill and were supposed to leave home for another night?!"

And in fact, the tone of the question was like the tone of the question that Newton asked himself before the discovery of the Earth's gravity, 'Why did the apple fall?'

A Country Called the World

Erki, "Actually, I wanted to deal with him severely the very next night. I thought logically and I found that I did not have any other choice."

The sheriff took his words seriously, but laughed and said, "So, your brother was kind of lucky! He owes it to nature!"

After the end of the late-night meeting, Erkie walked away from the sheriff's house and went home and the sheriff looked at him out of the window and said to himself, "You have always been a jerk and you still are. One can even figure it out just by watching your gait!"

Snow had begun to fall for about an hour. On his way home, Erkie opened up the collar of his coat a bit and took a few deep breaths and inhaled the freezing air with utmost delight. The joy of winning the argument with the sheriff and to convince him that he was right, gave him a feeling as if his whole being was filled with light and it was imminent that auroras would pop out of his eyes.

A Country Called the World

A Country Called the World

Saudi Arabia

At the School

The only thing that caused Walida to continue teaching at that school for a while was her mother's concern. After a long time of illiteracy, her mother had found a sign of great courage to learn reading and writing at the age of forty-seven and went to the classroom along with her daughter every day. The presence of a mother in a class of twenty-two seven-year-old kids was very weird and funny, especially since she was always more enthusiastic and active in the class in comparison to her classmates. Every night she asked her daughter to read her a book and tried to learn things in advance, such that while it was not yet three full months from the time that she had begun to learn how to read and write, she was eager to get into mathematics, medicine, and astronomy.

There was a graveyard near the school and incidentally, a number of its graves were located at the corner of the schoolyard. Every time someone died and there was a funeral procession, the children, upon hearing the sound of the people chanting *There is no God but Allah,* stared at the yard gate and waited to see whether the corpse was supposed to be buried in the school or not. However, nobody had been buried in the schoolyard during the ten years passing from the school's construction. The reason for the kids' expectation was certainly trusting in the school principal's statements. The school principal, to demonstrate the importance of study to the children, had made up a story – which was rather scary than instructive and motivational – and told it to them on the line-up.

– "Dear children! Education has a special place in God's kingdom. Education is so important and sacred that some humans make a will before death in order get buried in the schoolyard after death, to take part in the blessings of this holy place that is filled with goodness by the presence of people like you, and experience a bright and beautiful post-mortem world, to be protected from the horrors of the grave space. The study is important even after death."

In fact, Walida's mother was encouraged to study under the school principal's influence, whose speeches were broadcasted every day from the public-address speaker system that could be heard at their home.

Whatsoever, someday the school principal, who also owned the school's grounds and the village governor, had to agree on whether they were going to relocate the graves or attach a part of the schoolyard to the cemetery.

In the middle of the academic year, at the time when Walida's mother had partly learned how to read and write, she asked her daughter, "Do not you think I have learned enough reading and writing? I want to learn mathematics as soon as possible."

Walida was busy checking the children's spelling worksheets. She immediately drew a triangle, a square, and a circle on the paper and asked her mother to tell the name of the geometric shapes.

"Triangle, quadrangle, no angle," the mother replied earnestly.

Walida laughed loudly and pulled out her mother's spelling worksheet out of the paper stack and said, "Do not rush it! You will learn mathematics soon. Here you are! You have got the highest score." and for several times in a row, she saw her mother's tears of joy.

The sun had set. Walida got up and stretched and arched her body. The redness of the sky reminded her that she was supposed to have applied henna to her mother's hair. A little later, after dying her mother's black and white hair and turning it to red, began to check the sheets, which was not very time consuming but because Walida's mind was occupied, the correction of the sheets took a little longer. A bit later, the drowsiness caused by prolonged insomnia took Walida's large and black eyes and forced her to fall asleep on the sheets.

At the class, all of the kids received their papers and since the teacher was generous toward them, they were happy after all. One of the students by the name Hesham was absent and Walida decided to go to his home and give him the paper. The door to Hesham parent's house was next to the blackboard.

– "You are really a caring teacher. This way, please."

While Hesham's parents were warmly greeting Walida and expressed concern about their child's situation, the missing teacher, after walking through the labyrinth of numerous rooms in the house, arrived at the room where Hesham was.

The missing teacher patted the student's head and asked his parents mournfully, "What's up?"

Hesham's mother snatched the rosary from his wife's hand and said to Walida," Miss teacher! I have vowed, that if my son gets well, to give away charity meals as many as the number of the beads in this rosary every day....," suddenly she screamed, quivering with fear, and placed her head at the feet of her son.

A Country Called the World

Hesham's father rested his wife's head on his shoulder and told Walida's that his son has Malta fever. Then, Walida vaguely heard Hesham's voice, which resembled a man's voice, "Bury me in school because in that case, I will be comfortable. The others will study instead of me and I will progress effortlessly."

After they buried Hesham in the cemetery, the kids asked the missing principal why they had not buried him in school? The miss principal answered that it was no problem and Hesham's soul was certainly glad since he was buried near the school and would benefit enough of their education.

Walida had a vision that quite accidentally; they buried Hesham in a grave that was right behind the school wall. All the kids and also Walida's mother, holding strange books in hand, leaned on the wall that separated the school and the cemetery, and took turns to read aloud something that they had not yet been taught to read, to supposedly sooth Hesham's soul more and more.

– "Oh, my God! It seemed so real!"

It was midnight, and the mother had fallen asleep on her side, a little above Walida after she had thrown a blanket over her daughter. Walida decided to get up to drink water but she felt her right hand that she was sleeping on it, was much enlarged. So, she lay on her back for a while, and after her right hand woke up as well, went to drink the water. Drinking water doped up springtime in the endless garden of her brain, which had turned to autumn due to the nightmare, and it was enlivened again; and when she stood behind the window under the moonlight and a gentle breeze brought to her the smell of mother's eHannah-dyed hair, her heartbeat returned to normal.

In the morning, when the missing principal with her assistant checked the children's heads lest somebody's hair cut was longer than the thickness of her or her assistant's index fingers, the missing teacher entered the school with her mother. The mother went to the classroom with the other kids, but Walida told the principal that she had to talk to her in private for a few minutes.

At the principal's office, Walida, with a calm but serious tone, said to the principal, "You should not give speeches like that to the children anymore. The importance of study after death and the words you made up by yourself."

The miss principal sat down behind her desk and while leafing through tens of sheets on the table, replied, "You are a good teacher. But you are not entitled to address me like that. I feel it is reasonable to emphasize the importance of education to the kids in this manner."

Walida was upset by the principal's monotonous tone of voice and barked, "Do you scare children by the afterlife to encourage them to study? God help us!"

The principal hit the papers hard and jumped up from her seat.

Walida stood firmly against her and did not move a hair even when she was shouting just one step away from her, "I know what I am doing! It is none of your business! I am the principal! I own the premises!"

When the principal finished talking, Walida got out of her room and headed to the classroom at a fast pace. Other teachers came out of their classrooms due to the ruckus between the principal and Walida and stared at the end of the corridor where the principal office was located. Walida passed in front of them and reached her classroom.

A Country Called the World

"I will no longer stay here. Get up and come with me," she said to her mother.

The teachers stopped Walida in the yard, and the one who was more intimate with her, asked, "What is the matter? Did not they pay your wage? Or is it because of the graves? Wait! Believe me; we have repeatedly warned her that it is not right to have graves on the school premises. But she does not listen to us. The graves that are located in the schoolyard do not have any relatives since if they had, they would have complained about it and the principal had to comply."

Walida freed herself from her colleagues' grip, went toward the yard gate, and said, "I disagree with his statements, which, in his own words, are used to motivate the kids. Otherwise, it does not matter to me whether the graveyard is a part of the school or the school is a part of the graveyard."

One of the teachers said, "Just like that?! You are quitting because of that?"

The one who was intimate with Walida went toward her again, but Walida ignored her and walked out with her stunned mother.

The landscape of a bumpy dirt road with a zebra pattern overcast due to the sunlight shining through the palm trees did not look like a way that one could return to. It only demanded departure.

Several days after Walida left the graveyard school, she found a teaching job at another school outside her village, which was the best excuse to leave the village and go to Riyadh, because the new school was at a great distance from her village. Her mother, who no longer saw the principal and heard her voice, gave up the study and also forgot the little literacy she had acquired.

After twenty years, Walida returned to her village and went to school. Her old colleague was the new principal. The schoolyard had shrunk and there was no grave in it anymore. Upon her arrival at the school office, Walida saw the black-ribbon-decorated photo of the principal on the wall but, just in case, decided to ask about the situation from her former colleague, "Where is the missing principal?"

Her colleague glanced at the deceased principal's photo as a hint for Walida that the principal was dead. Then, as she was reading the Surah Al Fatihah along with Walida, took her hand and directed her to a corner of the yard. She stopped at the distance of two steps from the wall, pointed to the ground and said, "She is buried right here as set out in her will, sans tombstone."

A Country Called the World

A Country Called the World

Nigeria

6,20 PM to 8,00 PM

When an unknown and wealthy 25-year-old woman by the name Buchi arrived at the city, not quite a month had passed after her arrival that rumors began to circulate about her. For example, it was said that those who worked in her industrial shed were never permitted to get out of there and perhaps they tended to disappear, and anyone who worked there would become rich, or they said that Buchi was an organ trader and they harvested corpse members in her industrial shed. The most important thing that made people curious about Buchi was the need to know what was going on in the industrial shed and why only those who met the condition that Buchi had pinned up on the industrial shed's gate were allowed to work there. Because of expensive clothes and the strange personality, people called her *The Beast* and if anyone was missing from the town, they said he had been certainly *busted*. Buchi was a tall and skinny woman whose taciturnity was mostly attributed to her mysterious nature rather than her calmness. She spent all day and night in her large industrial shed and rarely stepped out. At the times when she walked across the town, she was never alone. People always saw her in the company of an old man, a woman, and a teenage boy.

One evening, when Buchi was walking with her pals, as usual, an untidy woman ran to her and before Buchi's fellows could stop her, reached her, grasped the Buchi shoulders on her blouse, and said, "Madam! My daughter is only six. Please give her back to me."

Bucchi smoothed out her dress and replied, "Your child is not with me."

The woman wept, "Maybe she is in your industrial shed."

Bucchi, "No dear. There is no child in my industrial shed. How many days have your child be missing?"

The woman rested her head on Laura's shoulder, the woman who accompanied Buchi, and said, "She went out of the house this morning and has not returned yet."

When the woman was convinced that her daughter had not gone to the industrial shed and walked away, the old man told Buchi that he knew the woman and that she had no children at all.

The next day, Buchi saw the woman again. This time, she approached Buchi quietly with a calm face and said, "Madam, please. . ."

Buchi interrupted her, "Believe me; your daughter is not with us."

Young woman, "Please let me work for you."

Buchi, "Has your daughter been found?"

After a few moments pause, the young woman said, "I do not have a daughter. I want to work in your industrial shed."

Buchi, "You must meet my industrial shed hiring requirements."

The old man who accompanied Buchi pulled out a sheet of paper from his pocket on which the hiring condition was written with large letters and showed it to the woman.

A Country Called the World

Without looking at it, the young woman said, "I know the condition. But no. I am not one of those people."

Buchi, "Have you been working before?"

The young woman pointed to the far away from the fruit shop and said, "There. He fired me about two weeks ago. His shop was robbed, and he fired *me*. But I did not steal. I tell lies, but I never steal, Madam. Believe me."

Buchi, "Well, you cannot work at my industrial shed, but you can escort me like my companions."

The young woman looked at the stylish clothes of Bouchi's entourage and asked, "Will you pay me for this companionship?"

Buchi glanced at her fellows' smiles and said, "You will not have any financial problems!"

Young woman, "What should I do?"

Bucchie, "Like my companions, report to the industrial shed at 6,20 PM to accompany me for a walk. At 8,00 PM, you will come with me to the industrial shed and return home. It is your everyday job."

The young woman's jaw dropped and she stared at the ground. Buchi put her hand under the woman's chin, lifted her head, kindly looked at her eyes and said, "Report to the industrial shed at 6,20 PM. Good evening."

It seemed that none of the Buchi's companions who were hired just a few days ago, and neither the young woman who was supposed to accompany her, were willing to tell anyone about their nice and well-paid job. However, Buchi had told them they could safely tell the truth in case anyone inquired about their job.

The next day, at about six o'clock in the evening, the young woman, while putting on her stylish and expensive clothes in the industrial shed's hallway on a raised platform, asked her colleague, "Why no sound is coming from the inside of the industrial shed, where is the madam?"

"She will be here soon," replied Laura.

After recruiting the young woman, in ten days, all of the townspeople, none of whom met the employment condition to work in the industrial shed, were hired as Buchni's escorts without the previous entourage's wage cuts. All of them, whether the old man who was hired as her first escort or the last youngster who died laughing because of his high wage at the end of his first work day, received equal and very high salaries. No one was in debt to anyone, and the town thrived. All people shut down their businesses at 5,30, dressed in beautiful clothes, and waited for Buchi in front of the industrial shed. Buchi began to walk along with all of them. The only people who did not escort Buchi were the children who, indifferent to Buchi and her fellows' parade, were playing games and the devil.

Three weeks after the people's companionship, two young men called Shula and Ben, who had just been released from jail, while Buchi and her entourage were walking, elbowed their way through the crowd and approached her, and Shula said, "Dear madam! We meet the hiring condition for your industrial shed!"

Buchy said with amazement, "Oh, really!"

A Country Called the World

"Yes, we fought with the stone factory owner who bullied us and seriously injured him. We served four years in prison for that," Shula said.

"Have you examined the employment condition thoroughly?" Buchi asked.

"Yes, yes," Shula answered.

"Report for work at my industrial shed tomorrow morning," Buchi said.

The people roared in a hubbub.

"Why do the people follow you?" asked Ben.

Buchi, "It is better for you not to know. Come to the industrial shed at eight o'clock tomorrow."

The two young people gladly looked at the crowd and went away. None of the town's greedy people wanted to tell the two young men that they could get a lot of money just by escorting Buchi. At night, after accompanying Buchi and away from the industrial shed, the people were enthusiastically listening to the town sheriff's speech and frequently approved it while he had not finished talking yet,

– "People! If they get hired at the industrial shed, most likely they will steal all of Buchi's attention. Do you know anyone who works at Buchi's industrial shed? If someone has been working there up to this time and before us, which we all know is unlikely, it is not important because it does not affect our income. But today we saw Buchi happily hired them young dudes for her industrial shed. What if their recruitment in the industrial shed reduces or even ruins our income?!"

Everyone agreed to find the two young men and finish them off.

A Country Called the World

"Those two are homeless. Search everywhere" commanded the sheriff.

It did not take long that some people took the two young men with their hands tied behind their backs, to the sheriff. Shula and Ben, unaware of the plot, looked at the crowd confusedly and with astonishment.

"So you want to go to the industrial shed!" fumed the sheriff.

Shula, "Is it a crime?"

Someone in the crowd shouted, "You fool! If you had committed a bloody crime, it would be better than to decide to go to the industrial shed!"

The sheriff jailed both of them. The next morning, Buchi, after a long and futile wait to meet Shula and Ben, went outside to walk and asked the people, "Has anyone seen them?"

A woman in the crowd answered, "Oh, madam! Those two sacked my home last night!"

Sheriff, "Those two were not natives of this town. We will catch them soon." Buchi took a deep breath and felt pity for the two young dudes. They missed such a great opportunity!

When the crowd scattered after escorting Bucchi, as soon as she opened the door to step into her industrial shed, the sheriff's deputy approached her quickly and said, "Excuse me, madam. I have a trip tomorrow."

"No problem," Buchi replied with a smile.

The sheriff's deputy, to make Buchi move away a bit from the gate of the industrial shed, said, "By the way, my colleagues tracked the two young men. We will surely catch them tomorrow," then hugged Buchi very sympathetically and pulled her back a little toward him and said, "We would like to thank you. Both I and the rest of the people."

When Buchi said goodbye to him and entered the industrial shed and proceeded to close the gate behind her, the sheriff put his foot inside and prevented her from closing it and pushed Buchi back with the gun. The other sheriff's assistant, who was hiding with him in the corridor, entered the industrial shed as well. Both were so amazed by what they saw in the industrial shed that they could not hear the knock on the gate, "Open! Otherwise, I will scream!"

The assistant who had distracted Buchi at the gate entered too.

In the industrial shed, there was a small house whose window opened to the hallway. The walls of the house were covered with photos of Buchi's husband and two children. Photos of different sizes. It was not surprising for the sheriff and his assistants to grow wings upon seeing an industrial shed with two hundred meters' surface area, in the middle of which, stacks of bank notes were piled up to the ceiling; and of course, they would not be surprised by their growing wings as much as they were amazed by the money. When they began to believe what they saw, the sheriff put the gun barrel on Buchi's head and said, "Read aloud the industrial shed's hiring condition to us once."

– "Only those individuals who have willingly quit their previous jobs will be hired at the industrial shed."

Sheriff, "There are no jobs in the town in the current situation, or if anyone has a job, he clings to it with his teeth and he would not quit his job no matter how much the going gets tough; because he does not know what will be his task in your industrial shed. I have heard that your answer to anyone who asked you 'If I quit my job, what should I do in your industrial shed?' Was, 'You give it up and you will not lose anything'. How could he trust you? Is it not true that you doctored the condition in a way that no one could enter the industrial shed ever?"

Buchi, "Anyone who quits a job based on his boss's bullying or low wages or for any reason other than laziness deserves the promotion. Also, if I did not say what he was going to do in the industrial shed, it was because I needed the person to quit his job because of the harassment and enormity he saw in his job and not because of the hefty amount of money in my industrial shed."

Sheriff, "And what if such a person could be found?"

Buchi, "I would have awarded him all the capital you see, and then I would have ended my life."

The sheriff asked, "What was the point of hiring escorts?" and addressed his assistants who were rolling in the money, "Come here you fools!"

Buchi, "I was a gold dealer in Lagos, but I lived the simplest life. My husband was a professional cook, who used to bake my birthday cake every year all by himself. The last time, that is, on my birthday seven months and twenty-two days ago, I was on a business trip during the two previous weeks. But as usual, in order to be with my family at the time of birth, I postponed many appointments and boarded the plane to go back. That day, when my husband returned from work, he went out with our two children to buy the ingredients to bake the cake from the shop and bake the cake. But they had an accident when they were on the way back from the shop. Police said my husband was driving under influence, but I did not believe it and I was sure that the truck driver was hired by an enemy of mine. So much for my happy ending! At the height of living a simple life, my family should be shattered like that. First my husband, and then my two children, died between 6,20 PM to 8,00 PM, respectively. . . I was depressed for a while and later, I came to this town.

"I go out during the hours that you know and take a walk in the town to avoid the traumatic memory stress. I do not need to keep company. But because those who do not have a good financial standing asked me to help them, I hired them as escorts just to make them feel they are actually doing something. This way, I could give them as much money as necessary to meet their needs, and until this very night, I had not paid attention to the fact that the whole townspeople were following me."

Sheriff, "Why did you come to this town and want to put your decision into action here?"

Buchi, "Because this is the town where several years ago, I quit my job and went to another town and began working in a goldsmith shop. The old man who always walks beside me was my boss, and that woman and a teenage boy are his daughter and grandson. When I returned here, first of all, I looked for my boss and when I realized he was a basket case, I hired him and his daughter and grandson for the purpose that you know."

There was the gunshot sound and Buchi collapsed to the floor. The sheriff's men ran toward the sheriff, and one of them laughed with a couple of banknotes in his hand, "Real deal! Genuine Federal Reserve notes! One can buy out the whole town with that amount!"

A Country Called the World

A Country Called the World

Poland

Revenge

Adam, a high school mathematics teacher in Warsaw, woke up cheerfully one day after his dismissal and got out of the house with the intention of finding a new job. He no longer had any concern to be in the classroom on time or God forbid, go to school with inadequate knowledge and get shocked by challenging questions of some of the students. However, he was always ready, and perhaps he thought about his former job as such to convince himself that he actually had no interest in the teaching job, and it was a good thing that he was fired. He walked slowly, carefully scanned his surroundings, and breathed with full awareness. During his five years as a teacher, he never had that sense of control over his as such. Therefore, he regretted why he had not resigned before he getting fired because of that fateful incident. He did not think too much about his capacities, and entered the first store he found that needed an employee and began to work without asking about the working hours and the wage. He thought that he could work the whole day at the store and switches his job if he found it undesirable and thus, he would finally discover what else he could do besides teaching via trial and error. He was tired of the teaching job and did not want to talk like educated people about work, society, nature, the world, and other topics anymore; so much so that even if someone asked him, 'Why do you think the time in the cities -crowded cities- passes so fast, but so slowly in the countryside?' he would certainly reply that he did not know. Or perhaps he did not even say that, and he would just shrug it off, while for such a simple question he had a myriad of solid and logical answers in mind, different than the other things that the inquirer had heard in his lifetime or was supposed to hear in the future.

After a week and spending time at jobs such as salesmanship, working at a gas station, hair saloon, tailor store, hospital, and bakery, he noticed that he was not interested in any job and even if he was supposed to die in poverty, he would not go for any of them.

He sat on the edge of the bed and thought about the teaching job and compared it with the occupations that he had experienced. The teaching job was the only occupation that tried his patience and annoyed him, and he was pleased that the verbal abuse by employers under whom he had worked (most of them were terribly foul-mouthed) did not upset him; this meant that he could not and would not endure the teaching job.

It was past 2: 00 AM. He rolled to one side to sleep, but after a few moments he opened his eyes again and said to himself, "Perhaps I was not angry with the employers' abuse because I knew that I would not stay in any of those jobs".

He firmly gripped his head between his hands and said, "The bloody teaching job," then he looked at his bookshelf in the dark and though he did not see the books, he knew where each one was. In his mind, he imagined that he has burned all his books.

In the next day, he woke up by hearing someone knocking on the door. When he opened the door, a teenage boy with a sad face and slightly blue under eyes, said, "Hi."

A Country Called the World

Adam hugged him without saying a word. Then he put his hand under his chin and lifted his head and said, "Oh is it not healed yet? Surely it is not painful, is it?"

The teenage boy shook his head no.

Adam interpreted the long silence of the young boy as a sign that he had certainly come to take revenge. So, Adam was ready to defend himself as he brought pieces of cake for himself and his guest. The boy took the piece of cake from his former teacher and said, "Thanks, Mr. Swatski."

And after he put the plate on the table and Adam took a seat, he said, "If you had offered an apology, I would have withdrawn my complaint. Did you know that?"

During his job as a teacher, Adam had never made a mistake, and for two consecutive years was chosen as the exemplary teacher in Warsaw high schools. So, he did not like to believe at all that he had committed a mistake and ruined his brilliant career background. For this reason, since the day he was fired from the school, he never felt regret or imagined that he had done something wrong and not only did not suffer pangs of conscience but he considered himself to be a holy and perfect person, who, based on his wholesomeness and privilege, could not be blamed or accused of wrongdoing even if he committed homicide. Therefore, he smiled at his guest and said, "André! I have always covered your back."

André had already heard that from another teacher who had said, 'Anyway, he has covered your back a lot of times and he is a prestigious guy. You should not have complained about him', and as he expected, Mr. Swatski himself also repeated the same statement. But André did not get angry, and to boost the impact of what he had already prepared to say to the teacher, he said indifferently, "You think because you treated me well, I should not protest when you made that mistake? Do you treat everyone like this? When you do wrong to someone and face his objection, you bring up the good things that you have done for that person so as not to apologize? Mr. Swatsky! I must say that your love for human beings is superficial. You treat people well just to show off your good manners. Perhaps, you want to set a new record in keeping cool and avoiding mistakes and maybe that is why you do not see your mistake as a mistake. Another point is that your love and kindness to human beings is like the employer's love for the employee. The employer deems himself entitled to trash the employee just because he provides him with work and salary."

Suddenly, Adam screamed with his high-pitched voice, "Stop!"

André tried hard not to laugh.

Adam knew his voice sounded ridiculous, but continued without lowering the volume of his voice, "Do you think I do not know things about myself? Do you think I do not know what a wicked and mean jerk I am? Dear boy, I am no longer a teacher! You see? I do not pretend anymore! Yes, I always pretended all my life. I pretended I was glad to see my cousin after years, but I did not like him at all. I pretended I had the best wife in the world, while I knew that I married her because my mother wanted to and I did not want to challenge her. I pretended that I was not upset when you, you and your friends, mocked me and I loved you to correct you to be useful people for the community while I hated every one of you!" he stopped talking and after a brief pause that emphasized his screwed up overall appearance, under his pushed back waistline and protruding neck, in his tiny eyes behind the spectacles which were much larger than his face, and in his legs that were pressed together under the fabric of his trousers which seemed narrow like the schoolchild's ruler, waved his skinny hands again in the air and said, "You see?! Right then, when I met you at the door, I pretended that I was sorry and I pitied you but that was not true, and I behaved like that because I was afraid of you seeking revenge. Pretending, pretending, and pretending! Do you want to hear more? Now get the hell out of my house."

André, who during that time was scrutinizing Adam's tone of voice and crazy moves, was very pleased that he had dared to tell those things to his former teacher.

When he got out of the house and went to his friends, he said with a smile, "I took my revenge on him," and told the story to his friends. His friends laughed at his skillful mimicking of the teacher and nobody paid attention to the content of his speech.

A Country Called the World

A Country Called the World

France

Her Most Valued Self

The weather, which in some of the days got so cold that forced people to wear gloves and winter clothing upon leaving their homes, as well as the very pale and long shadow of the Eiffel Tower throughout the day, clearly indicated it was late in the fall. It was almost 6,00 PM and the moon was visible in the sky but not as bright as it was at night. The sky was still bright and somewhat blue. At that time, if someone looked at the sky out of the Emily room's window, could easily see the lily, orange, and violet colors were slowly covering the sky from the west and have reached the middle of it, while on the east side, there were still whitish colors and even the ever-present smoke of the coal factory in the distance did not upset the beauty of that landscape.

When Emily arrived home, the blue color spread across the sky and only a small part of the sky seemed orange with a blue background. When she entered the house, her little brother and sister were busy solving a puzzle, and the parents were arguing. They had been arguing for a quarter of an hour, but it was not necessary for Emily to be present from the beginning of their quarrel to know what were they discussing so heatedly that their voice could be heard from the outside of the house. Repeated arguments, in all of which the initiator and the culprit was the mother. Emily ignored them, bent toward the solved puzzle that her sister was cheerfully showing her and after faking a smile, kissed her face and went toward her brother's puzzle, which he always finished later than his sister.

- "Well done, my little rats!"

Upon kissing them, she spotted their wheezing and stuffy noses. So, she cleaned both of their noses with a soft cloth and fed them cold medicine.

– "Once, just once, accept it was your fault!"

The father came out of the room with his hat in hand and left the house. The mother held her head between her hands and stared at the floor. Emily, who had taken the children to their room before the father came out, went to her mother. As soon as Emily sat beside the mother, she rested her head on her shoulder and cried. After a while, she wiped her tears and said to her daughter, "You are back so soon! Let's go sit in the kitchen and talk!"

The mother's 180-degree mood swing did not surprise Emily because it happened all the time. The abrupt mood changes from sadness and weeping to a smile that formed on the mother's face for $1/100^{th}$ of a second reassured Emily that her parents were accustomed to the quarrel and could not help it. Emily, while mostly needed to be alone rather than go on chatting, said, "It is better that you get some rest. We will talk later."

The mother got up immediately and after she lit up a cigar, said, "No, I need no rest," and while she went to the kitchen to splash some water on her hands and face, added loudly, "Let's get ready guys! We are going to take a walk! Yoo-hoo!"

By 'taking a walk', she meant going to visit the children's aunt. So the children, feeling happy by the prospect of meeting their male and female cousins, first picked up their new toys and then allowed Emily to put warm clothes on them.

Twenty minutes later, Emily was sitting in the kitchen, thinking about her situation in the last two hours.

David was an attractive dude, and at 23 years of age, was three years older than Emily. When Emily saw him at the cafe two days ago, she felt she had struck a balance and no longer had any problems in life. A few minutes later when David left the cafe with his friends, Emily felt a sense of happiness and pride washed over her body by seeing that David was tall like her. Two creatures, one with short hair, black stubble, puffy eyes and tall, next to another one named Emily with long hair and wearing a coat with the same color as the boy coat's color, were lovers in the Emily's cloud-like daydream and the cafe waiter, to disperse it, had to tell her repeatedly, "Miss! Miss! The cafe is closed. Dear Mademoiselle, miss . . ."

David had come to Paris to study social sciences at Sorbonne. His father and mother were both university professors and he was their only child. The following day, when Emily met David at the college and began to talk to him, she did not know that he was studying at Sorbonne too.

– "Mademoiselle! I am eager to see you again to talk more with you. Can I meet you at Le Café Fouquet's at 5:00 PM tomorrow?"

Emily promptly replied, "Of course!" as she tightly held her textbooks to her chest.

The rough voice and perfect teeth, the smile that highlighted the cheeks in a charming way, the drunken laugh that made David to hold up his face, eyes that shifted in a certain order in their sockets, an order that seemed to be exclusive just to David, a high forehead that pulled the eyebrows toward itself at times of wonder and adopted a slight wrinkle, a body whose muscles could be felt even under his coat . . . all of them were for Emily, because David was interested in her, too.

But the next day, when Emily went to the cafe, exactly a few steps before the cafe, put on her coat's hat, glanced inside the cafe, and passed in front of it without going in. On the way home, Emily thought to herself, 'How to make sure he will not dump me after a short while? There are many girls around him. No one knows, maybe he hooks up with a number of sluts at the same time. No! No! I have to think right. I should not make a decision based on emotions. I have seen him on the same day chatting and joking with other girls, so why should I get stuck to him and waste my precious time with him and permit my sentiments to be trampled?'

Based on such reasoning, Emily realized how much she loved life and herself and valued her life. However, from the moment she passed in front of the cafe until the moment she sat alone in the kitchen, a deep and short-lived nostalgia overwhelmed her, which she was sure was not serious and originated in her fancying David. She felt pride by remembering her decision not to enter the cafe an hour ago. So, she got up to go to a cafe alone and celebrate to pay homage to her own ego, which she loved very much. She heard the American Indian folk music and a little later the sound of footsteps of several people that hit the floor softly and rhythmically, which was not unusual for those hours of the day. Emily always wondered how a family with four children of different ages could be so happy that they celebrate and dance almost every evening. Emily goofily danced to the sound of their music and got out of the house.

A Country Called the World

A Country Called the World

India

The Flawless

Vikram walked at a quick pace to reach the Chhatrapati Shivaji Maharaj Terminus Railway Station and sat down on a chair. He put the backpack on his legs. It was still half an hour before the train arrived. Those who were near Vikram sometimes mentioned him in between their conversations due to his fashionable youth-appeal leather backpack. The leather backpack in his hand seemed as inappropriate as a deer in an abandoned house. The old man had not separated it from himself since the night before. It was tempting that before the train arrived, he could do what he had done the last night once more. So, regardless of prying eyes, brought out one the pair of the kids' shoes from the backpack and smelled it.

When he was eight, his mother took him to the only shoe vendor in their village to buy him a new pair of shoes on the occasion of the new academic year. The shoe seller did not have a shop and sold them on a cart as a street vendor. When the vendor saw Vikram, he said with a serious and accusing tone, "Are you not embarrassed to go shopping with your mother while you are this big as an adult?"

The mother smiled and explained her son was just eight-years-old.

The old man felt he was interested in himself more than ever. He wished he could find all the people who blamed him over the kids of his age, because of his early maturity and mistakes that he made and expected more from him, to thank every one of them. One of the pair of shoes reminded him of the first duties entrusted to him. At the same humble age, he went with his father to the hills around the village to graze several cows every day. In a winter day, when his father went to the forest to collect firewood, Vikram put the plan he had been working on for a long time to act and with much difficulty and effort separated a calf from its mother so to prevent the mother to attack him when he mounted it. As he mounted the calf, it spontaneously ran off to its mom and right at the top of the hill lost its balance, and it was just a few seconds after it had climbed the hill with much effort that it slipped on the other side and fell into the river. In the middle of the way, Vikram fell to the ground from the calf's back. He was beaten hard because of that mistake and spent the night in the barn without dinner.

The old man laughed about his pangs of conscience after his mistake. Remembering the three elements of curiosity, childhood, and naughtiness, intensified his laughter because they acquitted him of his mistakes.

He put one of the pair of shoes in the backpack and pulled out a piece of cloth which was the pocket of his father's shirt. When he smelled the piece of cloth, he remembered the anxiety caused by a mistake in his adolescence. At that time, he and his friends decided to raise money so that they could buy a baby bear. A wicked and cruel man had caught that baby bear for his own zoo. He realized that Vikram and his friends were trying to save the bear cub from him, so he suggested to them to buy the bear. The kids immediately began to raise the money. No one helped them apart from their families. Of course, they did not tell their families that they were going to buy the baby bear because the financial standing of their families did not allow them to easily spend money on such a task. In a short while, all provided their shares and waited for Vikram to contribute his share. Vikram had never asked his father for money, although he always helped his father as much as he could. He knew that even if he asked him, his father would not give him the money. Time and again, when Vikram returned home with his father from work, he said to him, 'If you do not pay me for work, at least by the things that I need by yourself.'

But the father neither purchased what he wanted nor paid him a wage.

The only thing that he said which pushed Vikram to utmost resentment and the verge of cursing him, was, 'I will save the money for you. Someday, you will realize what a great favor I have done to you by this.' Vikram never saw that day.

At midnight, Vikram tiptoed to his father's shirt and in the dark, took the amount he needed to save the baby bear and put the rest in his pocket. The bear cub had become very weak and skinny. Vikram was sure that the wicked guy had so many rare and large animals that he could not pay any attention to the baby bear at all. He and his friends saved the baby bear and released it back to nature. When Vikram returned home, he found his younger brother was beaten. His father was sure that Vikram had not robbed his pocket and trusted him completely.

The old man pitied his brother and as he put the piece of fabric inside the backpack, whispered to himself, "I always covered up his mess and supported him. Anyway, he had to somehow help me too. Eh?"

Shortly afterward, he pulled one of his high school books out of the backpack. When he smelled the book, all of the events that led him to take wrong decisions paraded before his eyes. He recalled his happiness in the last high school graduation days by the prospect of going to college and how much he hated school, especially the high school, and wished it had come to an end as soon as possible. He remembered the unsettling atmosphere of the family, whose members had experienced almost all kinds of crises. The death of his older brother because of drinking too much alcohol, the chronic major depressive disorder of his sister, the endless parental quarreling, the poverty and illness. He remembered that he had entered college just because of the academic atmosphere of the university and was not interested in his field of study.

At the late high school period, he was tired of his life more than any other period, and the thoughts and the tormented soul as a result of numerous problems had eroded his confidence and did not allow him to find his purpose in life. He just wanted to save his own ass. So, he entered the university, a campus in another city to get away from his family. That was one of the most misguided decisions he made.

After the previous night, he thought to himself at the train station that he could not solely blame himself in any way and suffer pangs of conscience because his academic years had put a great deal of pressure on his family. He thought, 'Why should I have felt guilty all of my life for my minutest mistakes?'

He had not asked that question from himself the previous night. Upon smelling the book, he felt at peace with his whole life and no longer needed to smell other junk that had remained for him from different periods of his life. Because the university years during which he dropped out was the most important part of his life, and just smelling that book was enough to justify all his past mistakes and to feel alright.

A Country Called the World

The sound of the approaching train was heard. The old man packed up and said, "I wish I had discovered this fifty year ago, not the last night, so as not to suffer so many pangs of conscience for my terrible mistakes! Or at least, I wish I had discovered that four years ago so that I could spend the recent four years with peace of mind. Many a day tasted bitter to me by the feeling of guilt and pointing the finger at this or that person. . ."

The old man was so deep in thought that he did not notice the arrival of the train and the people's ruckus who had crowded to welcome the passengers. Even when the train departed and the station was empty, he did not move from his seat. He hugged the backpack with his right hand, and put his other hand as a stiff pillar between his knee and chin, until his granddaughter, Karina, sat beside him and called him several times until the old man came to himself. Anyway, he had to cope with the regretful fact that he ought to have noticed what he had discovered the previous night, much earlier than that. He got up, took his granddaughter's hand, and after greeting her, walked home along with her. Karina was surprised to see his grandfather hugging the backpack with so much love.

A Country Called the World

A Country Called the World

New Zealand

The Fetus

After removing the bloody blanket from the bed, Julia helped the mother to lie down on the bed. She was very anxious and sweaty like her mother. The pale face, shaky chin, foaming mouth, grieving and nervous tics that had numbed the mother's toes and her abdominal pain had truly scared Julia. The mother moaned as soon as he rested her head on her pillow, "Bury it nice and slow."

Julia kissed her and went to the deep pit over which the mother had aborted her baby. She wrapped the fetus in a shawl, picked up the spade and began to dig a new pit in another corner. After five or six time shoveling, filled it again as if she had buried the fetus there. She ran to return the spade to the storeroom and wrapped the fetus in her shawl and carried it to her home.

Mr. Parker, Julia's father, was not interested in becoming a father and when he returned home after five months on the battlefield and found out that his wife, Linda, was pregnant, asked her to abort her child. Linda had not told him in the letter that she was pregnant, and afterward when her husband found out, she vehemently resisted his demand and did not agree to abort the child. But she submitted when Mr. Parker angrily reminded her, 'Once, I listened to you and you gave birth to Julia. This time, you must listen to me and abort this baby'. Therefore, on that day, Julia assisted her to walk a distance to get to the pit. A few days before the abortion, when she searched around the yard to find a place to bury the fetus, she saw a pit that her husband had dug to bury Julia's fetus eighteen years ago.

After Julia's departure, Linda, with all the feeling of guilt she felt in her heart due to the abortion, fell deeply asleep, and at the same moment a beautiful and large butterfly along with a gentle breeze entered the house and - clueless because of what it sensed around it was nothing but solid state - landed on the lily flower of a flower pot on the Linda room's windowsill. The butterfly saw that Julia hastily pulled the curtains of the windows of her home, so when her mother woke up, she could not see inside of her house.

Julia looked carefully at the 5-month-old fetus that easily fit in a palm like a red and shiny statue and many parts of its body had not grown yet. She wondered why women had to suffer to the brink of devastation to give birth to such an ugly creature. She thought to herself, 'How good it was if after taking action to have a baby, the baby suddenly appeared in front of the man and woman's eyes. Or, for example, they took action to have a baby tonight, and wake up tomorrow with the sound of the crying baby that could be heard from somewhere like amidst of unwashed clothes, on the kitchen table, in the henhouse, or the pigeon nest in the attic. This way, neither the belly swells abhorrently or there any birth pangs.'

When Julia saw the fetus, it seemed incredible to her that she had once been a fetus. How could a creature as small as one of a pair of men's shoes that was nothing but ugliness had turned to a tall and pretty girl? She looked at herself in the man-sized mirror next to the window. She looked at the fetus again.

– "No, I've never been as ugly as you."

A Country Called the World

She zeroed in on the fetus as if she was waiting for its reaction. She moved her head closer to it and said, "I've never been ugly like you!"

A moment later, she got up and stood up in front of the mirror. To prove to herself she was not only beautiful in clothes, but she also undressed completely naked. She meticulously examined herself from head to toe. She felt happy that she could not remember her fetal period. She put on her clothes and with her honey-colored eyes, looked at the window of the mother's room, at the large butterfly on the flower. Her mother was still asleep. Julia was suddenly taken aback with terror and looked at the fetus again. She thought, 'The fetus will grow up someday after all. It will be beautiful someday,' and with a humiliating smile, said to the fetus, "But at what cost! At the expense of your growth and beauty, your mother gets exhausted and worn out day after day, and your father will fight with anxiety every day until you grow up and proudly walk around and attract the boys to yourself and choose the largest Auckland's stockbreeder from among them, you see? You will be beautiful but at the cost of draining the other two! You will be a beautiful adult, but what is so special about you that your father and mother foolishly sacrifice their life for you? You are nothing but a waste of your father and mother's lifetime!"

The sound of the car followed by Andrew and his driver's laughter pulled Julia to the window. Julia waved for her husband and her husband sent her a kiss as usual. When he entered the house, he smelled an odor like leftover food and he commented, "What a stench!" then put the flower branch in his wife's blond hair. As Julia was patting Andrew's boney face and examined his brown eyes and golden eyebrows and hair, she could not wrap her mind around the fact that her husband has also been a fetus someday, and said, "We have a guest!"

Andrew was shocked by seeing the fetus. When his eyes fell on the fetus, he unconsciously removed his coat and put it on the fetus. Then he sat down, leaned back on the chair, clenched his right hand, and bit the back of his fingers sorrowfully.

"I am going to check on mom," said Julia awkwardly.

Andrew did not notice her departure. The fetus' stench did not hurt him. A moment later, he slowly and dolefully pushed his coat to the side. He could not stop his tears. He thought, 'Is there a person more brutal than Julia's father in the world?' Regretfully, he hit his head lightly a couple of times with his fists. Maybe if the stillborn baby had been born normally, it could succeed as an adult like Andrew and become an effective and useful person. Andrew whispered to the fetus while crying, "I am sorry," and then he got up and went out.

At Mr. Parker's home, Julia, with a glass of water in hand, said to her weeping mother, "There, there. . . it was a nightmare."

Linda could hardly speak due to intensive weeping, and said, "I am a murderer! It talked! It talked to me."

She pulled her head back in the opposite direction of Julia's bosom and rejected the glass like a kid reluctant to take bitter medicine. Julia brought the glass closer to her lips again and said, "You will get better, you had a nightmare."

Linda drank two glasses of water one after the other to get rid of her, and asked immediately afterward, "Did you bury it?"

Julia said, "I buried it near the apple tree, a bit farther than the pit that dad had dug for me," and added with a smile, "I am sensitive about my own pit! I like it," then rested the mother's head on her leg and to distract her from crying, added, "Shh! Keep your voice down! You look so beautiful!"

"I want to get up. I got tired. Help me," said Linda.

As soon as Julia grabbed her hand to help her out, she saw Andrew was coming toward her, and when Andrew asked her to step aside so he himself could help his mother-in-law, Julia sensed his grief by seeing his serious complexion but it was no reason that she could not have hinted, "Did you bury the fetus?"

Andrew pretended he had not heard it and did not answer her, and before Julia had a chance to repeat her question, Andrew began to greet his mother-in-law.

After the darkness fell and dinner was finished, Andrew pulled his wife to a corner, so after saying, "It is better to stay with your mother tonight," proceed to ask a question that had occupied his mind for a couple of hours, but Julia said, "I was already going to stay here tonight. Did you bury the fetus?"

Andrew, "You got tired so soon! I thought you wanted to keep it for a day."

Julia, "I just wanted to take a look at it. I apologize you for bringing the fetus home. It was today that I noticed you got very upset."

Andrew, "Do not you like us to have a baby yet?"

Julia, "I am sorry. Believe me, the thought of having a baby makes me sick."

Andrew, "You yourself told me to grant you a one-year grace period to get ready for pregnancy. You said if we were going to have children, I should wait for a year so both of us grow more mature."

A Country Called the World

Julia figured out what was Andrew going to say, and confusedly and nervously warned him with a loud voice, "Bring down your voice! The mother is awake and hears you."

"But you still do not like to have a baby," continued Andrew, indifferent to his wife's tone of voice, "Why when your mother aborted the fetus, did not you bury it, and brought it home? What did you want to make out of it?"

"Why do you like us to have a baby?" fumed Julia, and without waiting for his response, went to the mother's room and after kissing the mother's shoulders, said to her, "I will stay with you tonight."

"I feel better. You can go if you want to," said the mother.

"I will stay, good night," replied Julia and left the room and closed the door.

Andrew was standing at the same spot, playing with his pocket watch chain. Julia had used that tone of voice and went to her mother to give a chance to Andrew to find an answer. Therefore, she asked, "Ok, did you think well? Why you like us to have a baby?"

Andrew, "We adopt a child from the orphanage if you hate pregnancy and giving birth. I should have suggested this a year ago."

"Why?" asked Julia with a frustrated voice, and added after she noticed Andrew's long, "Is it not true that you want your child to fill your emptiness?"

Andrew, "I do not have any emptiness. I have got everything that I asked for in life."

A Country Called the World

Julia, "So you want to experience the pleasures that you have experienced in all stages of your life once again. How pleasing!"

Andrew did not know how to explain the fatherhood desire in his heart to his wife. Certainly, all of his wife's words were not bullocks and Andrew knew that. But the reasonable arguments that his wife had raised on that night against his urge for fatherhood, could not extinguish the fire of his love for having a baby.

Julia drew herself closer to Andrew and said sympathetically, "We are happy. Believe me."

Andrew gazed at the floor.

Julia continued boldly, "Admit that you have gaps that you think your child would fill. Admit that the gaps in your life are nothing but your unfulfilled dreams. Darling! Say you like to be a father, so someday your child can be like yourself. I am just talking about a child that at every stage of life is happy and full of life, like you. What will guarantee that? What if he takes the wrong turn? What if one day you realize he is nothing but trouble? Nothing but a drunkard and antisocial person?!" and after a brief pause, she added alarmingly, "Maybe you yourself are tired of life and you want to have a baby for diversity! If you are tired, that will not solve the problem. Surely, you cannot get rid of yourself like that. Are you tired of life?"

Andrew shook his head.

Julia said, "Oh that is a relief. Obviously, you are not and should not be tired of life. You are progressing every day and you cannot get tired of life. You do not need a child. *We* do not need a child. My dear, we have each other and a long road is awaiting us."

Andrew could not come up with a sound conclusion after weighing her wife's words and could not pretend that he had given up the fatherhood idea. Sometime after Julia's words, he went to deepen the pit that his wife had carelessly dug a few hours ago and buried the fetus, but again the question of why she did not bury the fetus and brought it home haunted him.

Linda recovered a week later and Julia recalled the maids to the house. Linda had dismissed them all before the abortion because she would be embarrassed if someone noticed her resentful deed. She did not even call the doctor.

Mr. Parker returned home two months after the abortion.

At night, Mr. Parker began drinking whiskey and telling about the events in a previous couple of months. At full-blown drunkenness, he reached the point that "Boom! And he was torn to pieces. I bet his comrades in the bunker did not mourn his death the way they had been upset by the fate of his child. Did not I tell you that? Andrew, please fill my glass. Yes. He had only one child. All his life! All his life, he had only one child and when he died; his only child was left alone. Before his dispatch, his wife took care of the child. And he! My Foe. In the last year on the front, he did not know that his wife had died a year ago and his son, who was just eight, was wandering in the streets. It was a year that he had just one person in the whole life. he was not aware of that! One of the POWs told me that. Haha! Haha!"

Andrew looked at her mother-in-law's face, in whose eyes tear had gathered. Julia was pissed off and looked at her father angrily and got up and went home.

A Country Called the World

Mr. Parker, asked after laughing boisterously for a moment, "Gone? Julia!" and as he looked questioningly at his wife and son-in-law, said smilingly, "it is her loss. I have not told you the real thing yet. Oh! What a night! Is there anyone happier than me?! Ho, ho! Do not you think it is funny? That boy, the one who was left alone, homeless and miserable! When he saw me, he said, 'Let me come to your house. I do everything you say, just give me shelter and food to eat. I will do with two light meals a day. I promise not to object even if I have to sleep in the barn,' he did not know I had killed his father! He did not let go of my legs. I traveled a few miles while he was sticking to my legs! What's more, I had just got used to him and I felt that if I could assume he is like an organ in my body, I could go on my way without being angry of him. Ha, ha! Ho, ho! He was like an organ in my body! Like. . ." he glanced at his pants' crotch and added, "Like my hand. Are you scared? No! You thought I would say like. . . like my legs! Look at their faces! Ha, ha! What a night!"

Later, after Mr. Parker slept, the house fell into a deep silence. After Andrew went through a bit of mental challenge, he finally asked Linda, "Could you take it if you had given birth to your child alive but he would have suffered the same fate of the boy whose story was told by Mr. Parker?"

"I do not know," Linda answered, unmoved by his question, "I just believe that one either should not have a child or if one has a child, it should not be aborted, even if only a few days pass from the formation of the embryo in her body. I do not know how to describe to you the torment that people like me experience after an abortion."

A Country Called the World

Andrew thought for a moment, looked at the clock, and said good night to Linda and went to his home. Linda held the key to solve his problem. Andrew was certain that Julia was equally afraid of abortion as much as she hated pregnancy and childbirth. Especially if Linda noticed her daughter's pregnancy, it was very unlikely that Julia attempted to abort the child afterward. Such an idea led Andrew to impregnate Julia the same night by getting her drunk.

Julia was very frightened when she noticed the signs of her pregnancy and told her mother about it. Andrew's plot worked! Julia was very angry and anxious about what had happened in the first few days, but she submitted to the status quo, fearing that her angst might destroy the fetus.

When the child was born, Julia felt very interested in it in contrast to what she had already thought. Perhaps because she had already discharged her anger and hatred on the fetus born from her mother, or maybe her maternal instinct had really brought her to her knees. It was a love and affection that did not even fit in her own beliefs and she did not know how to tell Andrew how much she loved their daughter.

When their daughter, Sarah, was four-year-old, Julia swore upon her birth that she had seen and felt every moment of the growing up of her child better than Andrew.

Andrew said, "Well! Of course, it is supposed to be like that! It was in your stomach."

Julia said, "Moreover, I sensed her face that was small and red like an adult man's fingertip in the cold up to this moment. . ." she kissed her daughter a few times in the arms of the grandmother, "Up to this moment with all my being."

A Country Called the World

Linda had unwittingly caused all that happiness and joy in the life of Julia and Andrew, in the dull atmosphere of her own and their family. If Julia had not seen her mother's situation after abortion, or if Linda had not scared Julia of abortion after Julia's pregnancy, Sarah would have been aborted too.

It was not important for any of them that Mr. Parker was not much interested in his granddaughter. Andrew, until the last day of his life – when he died at his home while reading a book for his numerous grandchildren – anytime Julia joked that 'You are finally a dad! You had your way after all!', still did not know how to express his desire for fatherhood to Julia.

One of the days, during Sarah's childhood days when Linda was chasing her granddaughter in the yard and Andrew and Julia looked at them with pleasure, Sarah surrendered to the grandmother after running for a long time and sat down right in the pit that once had been dug for her mother's abortion. Linda immediately picked her up and as she carried Sarah toward her daughter and son-in-law to have afternoon tea together, returned a few times and looked behind her at the pit and its surroundings. Andrew, who never knew that the pit had already been dug for his wife, looked at Mrs. Parker's worried face with surprise. Sarah was trying to escape from the grandmother's arms and the grandmother pretended that she could not resist her. Sarah ran to her parents with laughter and excitement.

"Be sure to fill that pit later," Julia said to Andrew, and as she opened her arms to embrace Sarah, thought that if she had aborted her, regardless of her mother's words, could she have forgiven herself for not having such a nice experience.

A Country Called the World

A Country Called the World

Italy

The Unique Mob

He slowly opened his eyes. There was no sign of the mess in the house. He felt great pain on one side of his hip. It was probably an hour that he had been unconscious. He had to go to the nearest clinic as soon as possible to find out what the virus had entered his body. With half-open eyes, he opened his mouth and tried to say a word, but he could not do it. It was extremely difficult for him to talk. As he had fallen on his face like a corpse, he reached for a booklet above his head. He slowly moved his fingers and struck the cover of the booklet. Next, he managed to finger tap rhythmically on the cover using both hands. Then, he tried to remember the face of the last person he had seen. The last person was the one who warned him the previous day that the boss was not kidding. Marino remembered his younger brother Luigi very well. He felt pride that even in that situation; he could remember important people or events in his own style. A long time ago, he had invented this method to challenge his own mind in order to make the best use of his high intelligence. The method worked like this, he deliberately did not fully keep in mind any subject that was very important to remember. This caused him to think more when he wanted to remember that subject later on. In this way, he forced his mind to work harder, so he would never feel proud of his high intelligence and get lazy. So, in the same feeble mood, he unconsciously thought about the least important subject, that is, Luigi's strange behavior. The thought of how his brother could behave in such a strange way brought a faint smile to his lips. For example, before Luigi talked about a bear, he first mimicked its sound, or if he wanted to say that he has caught a cold, he first sniffled. The weirdest case was the time they dismissed him from the office with curses and shouting. When Luigi was going to tell his close friends about it, he cursed and shouted and then told the story.

Marino remembered the previous day; when Luigi knocked the door of his house and he opened the door, then Luigi first he drew a finger gun and put it on his temple and then said, "The boss does not joke with anyone."

Marino removed his brother's hat from his head, kissed his almost bald scalp, and said, "Say hi to your boss and tell him I am not afraid of anything."

He damned himself at that point of contemplation. After the boss injected the cold virus into Marino's body, just moments before administering anesthesia, he said, "To make you understand I am not kidding, I injected you with a cold virus this time. The next time, I will come to you with anthrax virus and I will kill you."

The boss was so confident of his power that he expected Marino would spit out the formula without having to beat or torture him, or burning down his house. Clearly, his stooges could find the formula after a little search of the Marino's house, but the boss wanted to use his own style to get to what he needed.

Marino lied on his back and thought about the boss. Each of the boss's children shone brightly in their own professions. The three sons of the boss owned the best brewing, farming tools, and flour factories. But the boss's daughter owned a restaurant which was not *numero uno*. The best restaurant was owned by Marino and the restaurant of the boss's daughter was the second-ranking restaurant in the country.

A Country Called the World

He got up slowly. His body was fatigued. His right shoulder hit the wall and he winced. He leaned against the wall to walk to the bed and fell into a deep sleep.

The next morning, he woke up with a knock on the door. This time, the boss entered his house alone. Marino, who seemed to have forgotten what had happened yesterday, opened the door, yawned profusely and went back inside behind the boss. Marino behaved as if he had been accustomed to encountering such people, totally oblivious to the fact that it was a matter of life and death. After the boss sat on the coach, Marino walked to the window and pulled the curtain to the side. He saw the boss's men who stood under the window. He tried to spot his brother to wave to him, but he did not see him.

The boss looked at him and said, "I told the others to move a little bit behind me. Your brother is standing with them on this side of the house."

Marino, while repeating the words 'Luigi, Luigi', headed for the door but the boss grabbed his hand and said, "I told you, he is at this side of the house. After we finish our job, you can go open the door and see him. If you open the door now, you will be shot because I ordered my boys to shoot you without saying anything, if you open the door before me."

Marino sat opposite the boss. He looked around him and got up again. In front of the boss, he picked up one of his unwashed shirts and blew his nose a few times. He was a little dazed and the effect of anesthesia was still in his fragile body after several hours. He sat opposite the boss again and thought that if he sat there the whole day without saying a word; the stubborn boss would endure it so much so that Marino would become tired of it in the end. But Marino did not want to surrender in any way.

Therefore, he said with a ridiculous smile, "Excuse me, I have no time to entertain guests. I must go to my restaurant as soon as possible. I will have breakfast with my favorite staff over there."

The boss lit his pipe and smiled. The smile gradually grew to a burst of wild laughter and tears filled his eyes. After a while, his laughter gradually subsided by squeezing his drooping eyelids. He pulled out a toothpick from his pocket and tried to drive out the piece of meat stuck between his teeth, and a sound like the crackling of cocking the hammer of a Colt came out of his mouth. He was bored by playing nice with Marino. He pulled a large knife out of the backside of his pants and said, "I do not know what the people like you -who are not too numerous-see so special in themselves that makes them thick."

Marino clapped his hands and smiled, "I will never submit to bullying. Do you want the formula of my delicious dishes? Well, tell your daughter to come to me and respectfully ask me to help her."

Boss, "I have raised all my children as such, to take by force what they want in these cases."

Marino, "You see! I am ready to die, but will not let you have your way. Here you are, there it is. You can open my booklet and easily find the recipe for cooking the dishes. But no! You ruin your style this way. You want me to go to your daughter and kneel down and tell her the recipe with full consent. Fat chance!"

The boss narrowed his eyes and after a moment of pause, said, "Your brother has spilled out the gang's policy! Hasn't he?"

A Country Called the World

Marino, "No, no. He hates me so much that he joined your gang in order to be able to hurt me. I figured out your band's policy by myself. The fact that you have never killed anyone and just scare people to do what you want," Marino got up immediately and went to the door and continued, "Now, I will open the door and we will see that nothing happens."

He opened the door and stepped out of the house. All the gunmen pointed their weapons at him but no one fired. Marino saw his brother had turned his head away, as if not willing to see the scene of his brother's murder.

He laughed and said to his brother under his breath, "Clown talent!" then went back inside, closed the door, and said, "Yes! I opened the door and we saw that nothing happened. Not a bullet was shot; the weapons are designed for training! You hate murdering people. Your men set the stage really well to scare me, Luigi in particular!"

The boss wiped the sweat from his face and pulled out a pill that had been prescribed by the physician a while ago for his arrhythmia. Marino brought him some water and the boss swallowed the tablet and said while breathing with difficulty, "Look here, boy! You got it right. I want to get to the formula, but neither by opening your booklet nor by killing you. However, if you do not give me the formula the way I want it, be sure that I will choose to kill you in spite of the two other options!"

Marino, "Based on this, I will be the first person to be killed by you. The first one who ruins the policies and traditions prevailing for many years in your dynasty! By the way, how can you live the rest of your life after killing me? An inner voice will incessantly whisper under your ear that you have broken the rules! Afterward, killing people will become easy for you as a normal practice, and you will no longer be unique. Because you will be like other gangs of the Italian Mafia and you will lose your own style."

The boss, for whom being unique was a critical matter, started to beg, "Please! Do not discredit me in front of my daughter."

Marino, "Does your daughter know what you expect from me?"

Boss, "Yes. Of course, she knows. I told her that I would make you go and kneel and . . . "

Marino, "What if we do not do it your way? Tell your daughter to come to me so the three of us will talk about my restaurant's recipes."

Boss, "No! It is out of the question."

Marino, "If I have my way, you would have not achieved what you wanted just once. Ok! Choose. Do you like to be a murderer and no longer be unique, or would you prefer that only one person does not submit to your demand and all go well?"

Boss, "You will tell this to everybody."

Marino, "I promise not to say anything to anyone. I would be crazy to undermine the credit of a gang that my brother is a member of it. You know what; the main reason that my brother joined your band was your unique policy."

Boss, "Now, what do you want?"

Marino got up and put on his outdoors clothes. He combed his hair and said, "I have to go as soon as possible. Bring your daughter to my restaurant today and propose very respectfully."

Boss, "But what should I say to my daughter?"

Marino, "Tell her, from now on I am your family counselor, so your daughter will no longer disapprove why I did not give her the recipe the way that I should."

The boss had no other choice. He was even pleased in his heart to give a high position in his gang to such a clever guy. In fact, the boss recruited Luigi just because he was Marino's brother. He thought perhaps Marino's brother had inherited a bit of Marino's high intelligence. The boss accepted his offer and went away. After the boss and his men departed, Marino laughed all the way to the restaurant.

A Country Called the World

A Country Called the World

Sweden

Double Tears

Thomas, Emmanuel, and Camilla were three children of Eva. Thomas was a college student and his brother and sister studied in high school. Besides their curricula, all three had a great interest in the art of painting which was a source of dismay for their grumpy mother. Eva's husband had no objections to this matter and even the night that Eva's mouth quivered with anger and she said, 'Art will eventually undermine her study! O' God, spare my child this curse!' he had replied calmly, "Please do not bother Thomas. Leave the kids alone."

She sought excuses and picked quarrels and nagged in every situation and every day and even if something was done right but not in the way that she desired, it was discredited because of her accusations. Seldom did she calm down. The kids endured her maddening grumbles until once and for all, Thomas, the older child of the family, fought back against her nagging in a horrible way and showed Eva her real self, namely, what she should have been but was not. Thereafter, she gradually calmed down.

The first day that Thomas brought the painting canvas home - and in fact, it was he who caused his sixteen-year-old brother and fourteen-year-old sister discover the love for painting in themselves- and left the house, Eva went to his room and threw the canvas and art supplies to the floor and ruined them. Thomas returned home a little later and without asking who did it, found Eva opposite him with an angry face.

She said, "Art is a mirage that drowns the artist in," and continued with a peal of crazy laughter while clapping her hands, "I made up this phrase by myself, art is in our blood!"

Thomas cautiously picked up the small vantage statute of a goat that his mother had inherited from the past generations, from the three-legged table in front of his room and asked, "So, *you* did it?"

"Yes! I broke it, as a matter of course," shouted Eva.

She looked at the upset and worried faces of Emmanuel and Camilla and said, "Listen carefully! I will break anything that does not relate to your study. Even if I see a color pencil in this house, I will kick your asses."

Suddenly Thomas attacked his mother and smashed the statue against the floor at a very short distance from Eva and pulverized it. Next, at the same time that Eva screamed in fear and his sister began crying, he grabbed her mother's chin and looked into her eyes and said, "You are a person awash with complexes! Someone who has not fulfilled her wishes and cannot bear to see other people's successes at all. Someone who even when she wishes her children attain high positions through study, she pursues it just for her own sake because she has not achieved anything in life. What the hell do you want from these kids? Huh? To move up the ladder? I bet even if they attain a good and honorable position but do not become rich; you will still nag and harass them. You! A money-obsessed person, who does not want to believe that artists are successful people too. You! You are a loser! You ..."

Eve covered her ears, went into her room, and slammed the door shut. But as soon as she entered the room, the rest of the story was unlike what the kids imagined, that is, their mother allegedly sitting at a corner and crying. She was scared, but she had carefully listened to Thomas's words, who said, "You have taken refuge in your room?! When you see yourself in the looking glass, try to remember what a monster you are. It is not the kids' fault. Their only fault is being born into this family! Come to terms with your complexes and misfortunes and get off of our backs!"

He pounded on the room's door and left the house. Ten minutes after the atmosphere of the house calmed down, Camilla knocked on her mother room's door and said, "Mom, it's me. Open up."

"I am fine. Leave me alone. Soon, I will get out of the room and we will have lunch together," replied Eva.

Then she picked up the small bedside mirror and looked at herself. Thomas was right. Her wishes were buried in the wrinkles at the side of her eyes, and the trembling of her hands was nothing but the result of the paranoid thoughts and struggling to protect a cold and dull life in which, lest the children turn to machine-like humans. The whiteness of her hair-which was a symbol of toil to construct her life and experience and he was proud of each of its strands– screamed, 'you wasted your life!'

As the thoughts intensified, she pressed the mirror firmly on her legs and cried. She was weeping for herself and felt sympathy for herself. Not because she was unsuccessful in raising her children but rather because what she saw in the mirror was not her real self. she squeezed the mirror and looked at herself without a chance to have any objection, such as when someone looks at a toddler who has burnt the house down by its naughtiness and cannot blame it for its mistake. She could neither blame the middle-aged woman she saw in the mirror nor blame her child that why she had not seen him earlier before she had spent her youth so that he would speak to her as he did that day. Maybe if someone had told her long ago what Thomas had said on that day, later when she saw herself in the mirror, she would not wish to destroy herself and would not throw the mirror at a corner in a way that her children worriedly knock on her door and say, "Mom! Answer us."

Shortly afterward, Eva felt that while she was crying for herself, she was also shedding tears of joy and happiness for her son, Thomas. Because Thomas would turn into what he wanted, and whenever he saw himself in the mirror, he saw nothing but happiness and life. On the other hand, Eva was arrogant and did not want to behave in front of her children in the way to admit that she was not right and her way of life had been completely wrong. So, she left the room with a serious and upset face because of what Thomas had done and told her daughter, "Why are you staring at me? Clean up this mess fast."

A few days passed from that incident. Thomas was painting on a new canvas. Camilla was walking up the down and pretended that she was learning her lessons, but she was waiting for the door to Thomas's room to open and see the canvas, even if just to take a peek. Thomas was aware of her sister's enthusiasm to see what he had painted on the canvas. So, when he got out of the room to go to the bathroom, he left the door wide open and turned the canvas to face the door. Camilla's eyes were scanning the book and her ears were filled with her quarreling parents' noise, but her heart was restless to see his brother's painting. After the door to her brother's room was opened, she passed in front of the doorway a couple of times, and each time paused briefly.

A Country Called the World

Several eyes were painted amateurishly on the canvas, but since camellia knew nothing about painting, they looked like a masterpiece to her. She was extremely fascinated by seeing the watercolor and the whiteness of the canvas and as she walked the length and breadth of the house, imagined that she was standing and painting by a river, with short white sleeves and the suspenders of her checkered red pants are over her shoulders and her black hair is down to her waist. She was very excited by the fantasy that she imagined herself on the canvas, painting the landscape. A painting within a painting! She began to daydream again because she had forgotten to paint a pair of shoes for herself. Since the ground under her feet was grassland, she thought it was better to be barefooted. Barefoot, with the bottom of her pants folded up a handbreadth. Thomas returned to his room and saw his sister was walking up and down the room deep in thought and guessed she was seriously engaged in her textbook and did not pass in front of her room. But as soon as he was going to close the door, he saw her approaching him at a fast pace. She told him excitedly, "I feel I like the painting!" then she lowered her voice and added for more emphasis, "I really do think so."

Eva was washing the dishes and, as usual, she was harassing her poor husband for the puniest and simplest things. On that day, she had inflicted bruises on the innocent body of her husband's leisure time with the whips of her nagging, saying, "Why, a few nights ago at the party, did you tell me to wipe the corner of my mouth in front of everybody? Huh? Did you want to ruin me? Do you think I have never eaten cake?"

"Darling, I whispered under your ear. If I had not said it, others might have noticed and laughed at you."

Eva, "So, what - those friends of your college days who were standing near us- were laughing at?"

"They did not hear me over the noise of the crowd," replied his husband.

Eve, "Goddamn others. Why do you think we should live for others?"

His husband was going mad and said regretfully, "I never thought that way!"

Eva pointed at the outside of the kitchen, "Here it is! Our daughter is the witness! Camellia! Hey."

Camellia immediately moved away from the front of her brother's room and went toward them.

"Did not your father just say 'I told you to wipe your mouth because you may be subject to others' ridicule'?" said Eva.

Her mother shut up as soon as Emmanuel turned the key and entered the house. Sometimes, Emmanuel faked sick or fought with someone at school, got battered, and returned home with a wounded face and torn clothes to calm down the mother and distract her from arguing with others. Therefore, his mother paid all her attention to him and her mind was busy for a few days caring for him. It was a while that Emmanuel had decided to stop faking sickness altogether and only fight and return home beaten up. Because when he faked ill, just headache and fatigue was not enough and did not impress his mother, so he had to drop in some fainting and chills too; up to the time that his mother was hell-bent to take him to a neurologist. Thus, from that day onward, Emmanuel focused only on fighting.

Eve went toward Emmanuel, and Emmanuel pretended to be more miserable and injured than he actually was. Thomas's parents took him to the bathroom to change his clothes and wash his hands and face and his superficial wounds.

He winced, "Ouch, ouch! My hand hurts a lot," and added with tearful eyes, "easy, easy!"

The tranquility that Emmanuel's trick brought to their home, made him feel proud of what he had done and forget the enormity of the whole mess that he had to invoke one of the bullies at the school by swearing to get himself battered. Emmanuel never told anyone, even his brother and sister, that he intentionally initiated the fight or faked illness.

Camellia, who was already crying and pitifully looked at her brother's wounded hand and soiled face, entered his room and sat down on the bedside chair.

Camellia, "Your face has purple on it! And green! And red! You always look like a painting when you fight."

Emmanuel laughed and tried to lean on his elbow, but he pretended to feel great pain and returned back to his place. Camellia partly raised from her chair but sat down on again and said with a sympathetic voice, "You will be alright soon."

Emanuel, "Do you like painting?"

Camellia exclaimed "A lot!" then pulled her chair closer to the bed and said, "Unbeknownst to mom, I examined the painting canvas and the colors and eyes that Thomas had painted on the canvas. Thomas will become a skilled painter. The eyes he had painted were no different than the real ones! I wish I could start painting too and have a painting canvas in my room."

Emmanuel, "Cannot you paint without a canvas?"

Camellia replied, "Of course not," and added, "Do you mean to paint in my booklet?! Huh? I do not know. Perhaps I will. But no! Every now and then, mom sneaks into my room on the pretext of cleaning house. She thinks I do not know that she touches my books and booklets. If she finds a painted paper in my room....!"

Emmanuel faked a cough.

"I go now. You get some rest. Let's talk about it later," said Camellia.

Emmanuel regretted his cough. He did not cough to force his sister out of the room, but to prevent her suspect his pretension. He was allegedly sick and needed rest, so he should not have talked like healthy people and asks her with his usual and persistent tone, 'Do you like painting?' However, his face was bruised and wounded enough to make-believe he was injured.

A month later, on a day that Eva returned home after a walk in the park, she saw Camellia was painting. She was very upset but did not say anything. Her anger was because she thought Thomas had allowed Camellia to paint on his canvas and is going to coerce his sister into painting. A few days later, Thomas bought a painting canvas for Camellia, which made Eva twice as upset but she did not say anything yet and, in response to her daughter who condoled her by saying, 'I promise to paint just half an hour a day,' replied carelessly, 'Do whatever you want,' and decided to play it cool to see whether her daughter really liked painting or not.

There was no longer someone to watch her nagging her husband and to sympathize with her and pay attention to her to reduce the tension and fill her ears every day with her repeated statements and complaints. As usual, Eva first began complaining furiously about her husband and children and life and then, when Camellia sympathetically sat beside her, she calmed down and went on complaining quietly and cried to attract more attention and, as far as she could, pretended to be innocent and hurt, so that her only daughter would pretend that she was right, just to make her feel better.

Eva was slightly jealous by seeing that Camellia was busy painting and could not control herself like the early days of purchasing the canvas and go to her room less frequently to paint. Her nagging of her husband has subsided and its duration was less as well. She was officially alone. She wanted to leave home forever and get out of Malmö. She felt that the kids did not need her anymore. The children were so scared of her that even Eva herself could not believe she had become such a dreadful monster.

Eight months passed from her fight with Thomas. During that period, Eva did not speak a word to her son and did not check out the rooms of any of her children. Eva's grumbling and complaints disappeared a few days after Thomas bought the canvas for her sister, but she still had kept her nervous and violent appearance. Her husband was delighted that Eva was calm and the home was peaceful. He thought the calmness was a blessing of the art that had arrived at their house. But in fact, Eva was depressed and so indifferent to her surroundings that she did not realize shortly after Camellia began painting, Emmanuel also came home with a canvas. The kids were very entertained. Emmanuel and Camellia went to school with their brother and everyone was happy that there was no longer a medium- height woman with gray hair and wrinkled face and the eyes that always suspiciously examined her surroundings, and she was replaced with a woman who was calm and does not pay attention to them and just with an angry face is constantly busy cleaning the house, walking, and sleeping. Eva was deep into herself. She went to Camilla's room after a long time and was nearly shocked to death by the joy of seeing her daughter's painting, but no matter how intense her joy was, it could not beat her serious complexion. So, without saying anything or nodding in front of her daughter to show her pleasure of her work, got out of her room and went to her own room. Due to the smell of paint and crumpled pieces of paper thrown around the house, the atmosphere of home felt unknown to her and the only place that was still familiar to her and somehow had turned to her own fortress was the kitchen. The artistic atmosphere that penetrated the house by Thomas's feeble arms and easily conquered Eve's selfishness, to the same amount that it was delightful and cheered up the life of the kids, obscured Eva's black and white life even more.

Camellia and Emanuel were in Thomas's room with their canvas to paint together. Eva had left the door to her room slightly open to hear their voices. She repeatedly cried tears of both joy and sorrow over the past months. She cried for herself as if she had been rejected besides being lonely, and also she cried for the joy of the courage of her children who pursued their own interests. But she had to do something; otherwise, she would die of grief. She had to really put her pride aside and make friends with her children or wear out in her loneliness.

A little later, the children's sound of laughter, the sound of the brush that soothed her mind when it touched the canvas, and thinking about painful isolation and the wishes that were gone with the wind, encouraged Eva to wipe her tears and go to meet her children. She went toward Thomas without saying a word, took the brush from his hand, and then went toward Camilla's

canvas and using Emmanuel's black watercolor paint, painted a
house like a child.

A Country Called the World

A Country Called the World

Greece

Cornelius, a Descendant of Socrates

One day after graduation, young Cornelius combed through a large part of Larissa to find a job and checked a lot of legal offices and met some of the Justice Department's judges. However, on that day he could talk to only one of the judges but he met many lawyers.

Around noon, after washing his hand and face with the cool water in the park, he sat on a bench, opened his arms and leaned his head back. A calm breeze had slightly moderated the intolerable summer for the people. Cornelius enjoyed the breeze across his face. It was quite a while that he had learned to enjoy his life at all times and be happy and live without complaining about the conditions. However, he was in that mood whenever he was alone, and in the presence of others -especially the family– pretended to be dissatisfied and upset. But later, he decided to behave everywhere as he was in solitude.

He opened his eyes and watched the slow dance of the tree leaves in reverse. A few seconds later, he put his hands in his lap and straightened up, took out the chicken sandwich from the bag and ate it with utmost pleasure. He ate so joyfully as if he was spending the last day of his life. After napping for about twenty minutes under the shade of the trees, he got up, splashed water on his face and began to search again.

He wondered at dusk, 'How many places I checked today? Three, four. . . seven. Seven places!"

When he returned home and opened the door and loudly declared, "Hello! I am home!" his stepfather was repairing the bedroom's door which his son had angrily and desperately pounded the night before.

He replied without turning back to look at Cornelius, "Welcome! Look. What is your opinion?!"

Cornelius went closer, touched the door, and said, "It does not look damaged at all. But I think its paint is not set yet. Where is the mom?"

The mother had gone out with Cornelius's brother to talk to him and alleviate his despair.

A few days passed while Cornelius checked all the offices in the town, but he could not land a job and he decided to go to Athens.

He was about to tell his decision at the time of having dinner with the family. But the atmosphere of the home was very silent and clearly, the way the mother, father, and brother looked at him meant they had agreed upon an unpleasant matter and we're going to tell Cornelius about it. Of course, Cornelius had predicted the arrival of such an occasion.

Before the family had a chance to talk, Cornelius said with a smile that was not faked at all and came straight from his heart, "You are the best chef in the world! Please pour some more meat for me again!"

The mother filled his plate without any reaction. Then, she gestured with her eyes to her husband to tell the matter to Cornelius but the husband rejected to do so and entrusted this duty to herself. Cornelius had deliberately lowered his head so that they could talk more easily using body language. After the father and brother compellingly gestured to mother that it was better than she talked first, the mother said, "How was it today, Cornelius?"

Cornelius, "Perfect! There is no other place that I have left unchecked. I ended up meeting Ms. Samaras the wife of father's colleague. As dad said, she was not a kind and compassionate woman at all. She did not want to work with any young person and give him easy cases. She was very greedy. There were so many files on her table that I swear they could keep five young graduates busy. Well! It was pure chance that I realized there was a great lawyer in Athens who holds an employment exam for graduated young people every year. I have decided to go to Athens. I will go tomorrow. I am sure I will pass the test."

"That is great. You will finally make it . . . but . . . but there is something you should know . . ." said the mother with a fake smile, unconcerned about what incident had brought that test into Cornelius's attention.

Cornelius's brother interrupted her words and said impatiently, "Do you want to say something or you are going to drag your feet till tomorrow by but… but…!" then, he looked at Cornelius and said, "We doubt that you have been really looking for the job in the recent days. Mother and father are almost certain, but I am perfectly sure you did not look for a job."

Cornelius knew why they were skeptical, but he pretended to be surprised by his brother's words and said, "I do not know why you do not believe I have been looking for a job in the past days!"

Before the brother starts to talk, the mother said with a calm voice, "Because you do not look like searching for a job, we do not see any signs of fatigue and frustration, no grumbling and complaining either."

Cornelius said with a smile, "I do not understand what you mean, that is, since I have no complaints and I am not desperate and depressed and do not feel sorry, it means that I am lying?!"

Father, "No, no. We do not mean that. Your mother is going to say that a person who does not have a job and is looking for a job, is usually tired and depressed. Especially, when he does not find the job after searching for two days, he curses the heaven and earth, but you are not like that. I personally think that you were not diligently looking for a job but you were mostly thinking about enjoying the sunlight, fooling around, and having fun."

Mother and brother confirmed the father's words as well.

Cornelius said with a serious tone, "Imagine two people are looking for a job. One is happy and the other, sad. They have the same problem. In the end, after a few days, none of them lands a job. The one who was upset by the lack of a job gets unhappier, and the one who was happy maintains his happiness and joy. Intoxicated by life! From your point of view, the one who has become sad and sorry deserves attention because he has put his back into finding the job. By attention, I mean 'do not worry, you will finally get the job, take it easy, do not push yourself so hard, etc.', But you are suspicious of the one who is not sad! Do you like him to be upset, too?"

Father, "No, it is not like that. You are wrong to the core. Someone who does not have a job cannot be happy, because he does not have money and cannot fill his stomach."

Cornelius, "I perfectly agree with you on this matter! I am always happy because I am never hungry and I have a shelter. I have no reason to worry because I have the basic things in life, which are food and a roof. Now, do you want me to feel inferior to what I am? I ask myself could I still be happy if I had no roof and I was hungry. Of course not. But now that I am in such a position, why should not I feel happy? Now that I have a roof and food and the specialty, why should I not enjoy life? What special event should I expect in life to start enjoying life after that? You mean I should feel unhappy until that special event occurs in my life? Please pay attention, my dears! You unwittingly behave as such, that is, you take depression and discomfort as a sign of feeling responsible. As if a person who is more upset and sad when solving his problems feels more responsible from your point of view, and even if he does not solve the problem, you do not pick on him. I have already tried this. I have already pretended to be sad and learned how accountable do you think I am."

Father, "But if you never feel upset and sad, others do not believe you have a problem in life."

Cornelius, "This is *their* problem, not mine."

Father, "Say, for example, those places that you checked for the job, if they found you sad and upset, you could have probably landed a job."

Cornelius, "I cannot pretend I am not me and get a job by stimulating their pity. Huh! In your opinion, more discomfort is the key to solve a problem! No, no, I will never be like that. I have found my way in life and the good news is that you will never see me sad. It is just enough that those who are in on it, see my talent in order to have the opportunity to flourish and grow. I will soon find such an opportunity."

Mother, "Are you ready to work in a job other than what you have studied for if you do not pass the test you are waiting for?"

A Country Called the World

Cornelius, "No way."

Mother, "Even if it means you must wait for an opportunity to flourish until the end of your life?"

Cornelius, "I am not going to look for an opportunity to flourish until the end of my life."

Mother, "I hope so. But if you do not find the job that you like, I advise you to have a career other than what you have studied for."

Cornelius, "Why?"

Mother, "Because it is nothing better than having no job. Believe me, half a loaf is better than nothing!"

Cornelius, "You do not know how much I hate this phrase! I often prefer nothing to many things. You have not forgotten why your beloved cousin's back was bent like this? And unfortunately, he became a symbol of responsibility! Yes, because he was a dock worker and it was not quite four months that his back was bent under heavy work. Before he got into that job, I told him to find an easier job. He said, 'There is no job, and no matter what this job means, half a loaf is better than nothing', and we saw how it was better than nothing!"

Brother, "You look only at the empty half of the glass. I know very successful people who have entered a career merely because that job was better than nothing."

Cornelius, "No, I do not look at the negative side only. The fact is, if a person deeply likes his career, it is impossible for him to do any other work. And even if he does, he will wear out after a while. In no circumstances, he would allow himself to stay away from his love, because otherwise, perhaps he will succeed in a job other than what he likes and earn a good income, but at the end of each day, he is not satisfied with his job in his heart and will not be happy. I do not allow that *nothing* deceives me, so I do anything to escape it."

Father, "Ok. You know yourself better."

Cornelius, "We left the dinner half-eaten! However, I am full."

He got up and before going to his room, said, "Do not worry dears! The key to the test that I am going to pass is intelligence and literacy, not a sad face!"

When he lay down on the bed and laughed at the thoughts that had come into his mind at dinner time. He was about to stand up at the dinner table and shout, 'Do you want me to be sad and depressed and angry?' Then rush to the window and break it with his fist, knowing that such an attempt would seriously damage his boney hand. Then, with a bloody hand, in sheer amazement of the family, and of course, with faked anger and fury go to his room and slam the door shut behind him and shout again "I no longer leave this room because I am deeply depressed and disappointed!"

A Country Called the World

A Country Called the World

South Africa

The Leap Year

Nadine was the sister of Mr. Bateson's mother, but since Mr. Bateson's children had never met their grandmothers, they called her 'grandmother'. She was a woman of eighty-one years of age and lived alone. After being barren for a long time, she gave birth to a daughter in her middle age but her child caught a high fever when she was not quite two-year-old and died and then her husband suddenly left the home and deserted her.

It was three years after the time that Mr. Bateson had asked his aunt to come to Pretoria to live with them. As soon as his twins were born, he brought Nadine to his house to be near his postpartum spouse and to help her out more or less. After the recovery, Ms. Bateson did not allow Nadine to leave their home. She pitied the old and lonely Nadine. Moreover, Nadine did not want to go back home because she was accustomed to them and also it was hard for her to continue living alone anymore. Dennis and Steve, the sons of Mr. Bateson, loved Nadine and most of the time when Nadine wanted to go somewhere alone, they accompanied her. Their company relieved Nadine of her desperation. One of Nadine's most enjoyable times was when she coordinated with Ms. Bateson that after she left the house, Ms. Bateson informs Denis and Steve. Then, before Nadine could go far from the house, she felt two small hands in her left and right hands and her soul soared over the joy of the fabricated surprise.

A Country Called the World

The New Year was at hand. A couple of nights before the New Year, the parents came home with the pine tree and all were supposed to decorate the house together.

Mr. Bateson, "By the way, the New Year is a leap year!"

His wife was disentangling the twisted wires of the pine tree lights and observed excitedly, "It means that our child will be born in a leap year!"

Mr. Bateson climbed down the ladder and said, "I am counting seconds for the arrival of the New Year," then went toward his wife. They wanted to go to their room as they kissed each other, but Mr. Bateson saw Nadine, who had fallen belly up on the floor. The kids were playing on her both sides and thought the grandmother had faked death to play with them.

Nadine felt a hand under her head. She heard the sounds more or less but the environment still looked blurry in her eyes. She tried to maintain her awareness but her tiny eyes could not keep her heavy eyelids open. It was quite a while that she had exerted such a force to do something, the power to stop her eyes from closing. Thirty-five years passed from the time that Nadine had lost her son. That year was a leap year with all its hardship and misfortune and even if Nadine did not lose her child, it was unlikely that when she was alone, she would not remember the terrible events of that year more than other events of her life. A year in which her jaw broke, her house caught fire, her nephew died, her brother went insane, her spouse left her, and worst of all, and she lost her child.

A few minutes later, she saw the faces of the physician and Ms. Bateson in front of her eyes. They left her alone in the room to get some rest. She recovered soon but she was very upset. She rarely talked and was no longer as friendly with the Bateson family as before. She could not stand the kids and went out of the home very early in the morning and after walking a long distance which was not good for her in that age, returned home without drinking water or eating food. Nadine finally made her decision just one and a half day short of the New Year. In any case, she did not have a good memory of the leap year and she could not bear it, no matter how she challenged herself. She was absolutely unaware of the leap years in the past since no one cared about them in her village and even if someone knew, he would never tell Nadine. But this time the situation was really different. She had to do something to distract herself from the fact that the coming year was a leap year. She first decided to deafen her ears and blind her eyes but she was scared. Then she realized that faking deafness and blindness makes others treat her differently to some extent and leave her alone in the private space she chose to live in. After she realized that the next year was a leap year, her private space was the empty room next to the storage room where no noise could be heard when she was in there. Therefore, if Nadine faked deafness and blindness, the family members did not care whether she was in her private place or in the crowd and since she preferred her privacy to any other place, they would have left her alone. By this trick, she could spend the leap year without leaving the room. However, she thought later that if the kids frighten her in that situation, her fake deafness would be easily spoiled. Therefore, she decided to only fake blindness. With the help of the blindness, she could boldly insist on her isolationism and decide to go through the leap year in the room next to the storage room. So, one day before the New Year, she practiced a little to know whether it was better to keep her eyes open or closed and when she felt sleepy and uncomfortable with closed eyes, she decided to fake blindness with wide open eyes.

Mr. Bateson took Nadine to her room with the help of his wife, and said, "Dear aunt, you do not need to be upset. Calm down and rest assured that we are going to your room."

Nadine was reluctant and said repeatedly, "My room! Take me to my room."

Upon entering the said room, Mr. Bateson said, "Sit down slowly. We have brought a bed for you."

Nadine lay down on the bed and said, "Close the door, please."

Her excessive discomfort left no choice other than obedience for the Bateson couple. The physician had told Mr. Bateson that the symptoms showed that Nadine's eyes were weak but not to the extent that she could not see at all and she should not be blind. He also told them it would be better to take her to other specialists, but Mr. Bateson and his wife did not take the doctor's advice seriously and we're sure she was blind.

A few minutes to the New Year, Ms. Bateson went to Nadine's room to tell her the New Year was near and ask whether she wanted to join the family gathering and that the kids were missing her hugely. But when she saw Nadine was asleep, closed the door and went away without saying a word. Nadine was actually asleep and woke up by the sound of the door closing. When she made sure no one was supposed to come to her room for at least at the turn of the year, she covered her ears tightly and closed her eyes and with a closed mouth, emitted a weak and nonstop screech out of the throat. Therefore, she did not notice the joy of the Bateson family and the turn of the year and felt that she was still in the previous year.

A Country Called the World

After the New Year's atmosphere subsided and the people returned to their normal lives, Nadine called Ms. Bateson from her room, "Take me to the yard."

Nadine stepped out of the house after a month. She took a deep breath. She felt she was released from jail and had entered another one. For her, not feeling that ominous year worth a year of faking blindness and tolerating a harsh life.

Six months and eleven days passed from the beginning of the leap year. One morning, Mr. Bateson returned home after several consecutive days working in a mine a few miles away from his home. He was supposed to install a long swing for the kids on the tree and then go with his pregnant wife to the doctor's office to check the status of his child. Nadine leaned on the wall and her stick to walking from her room to the yard. Mr. Bateson found a long rope and a medium-sized wooden seat and assembled the swing for his children within half an hour. Nadine sat on the chair in the yard.

"Hold the rope tight!" said Mr. Bateson, and pushed on the rope. Steve shrieked excitedly. Mr. Bateson kissed his aunt's face and went inside to go to the physician's office with his wife after taking a shower. Nadine was erroneously tempted to go near Steve to push him but she immediately came to herself and, although under enticement, controlled herself and overcame the temptation by remembering that the leap year was an ominous year for her.

Steve was swinging and in every turn, said with his cute voice, "Grandma! Yoo-hoo! Grandma! Yoo-hoo!"

Nadine was looking at him and had grasped the chair hand rest tightly lest she rushes toward him. Steve had bent his head backward so much that he could easily see Nadine.

A Country Called the World

– "Grandma, you look upside down! Ha, ha."

Nadine was going to say, "Be careful! Don't! It is dangerous."

Moments later, Steve lost his grip and fell on his back to the ground. Nadine perfectly saw the scene of his fall. She looked around her. No one was there. Steve fell completely fell from the swing and did not move. Nadine wanted to go toward him, but it would cost her a lot if anyone saw her, even if she could save Steve' life. Therefore, she went inside and yelled with a prolonged shout "Steve!"

Mr. Bateson ran out of the bathroom with a towel and before his wife stumbled and fell on the ground while rushing toward Steve, lifted Steve and took him inside.

Steve was fine. He was just startled. A bit later, he came round and was going to swing again. But the baby inside Ms. Bateson's belly perished. Mr. Bateson and his wife were very upset because they wanted to have their child born in a leap year. Nadine was still faking blindness and after Mr. Bateson and his wife returned from the hospital, she replied in response to Ms. Bateson who asked her how she had noticed Steve's fall, "Steve's voice was suddenly muted and I thought something bad must have happened."

A Country Called the World

Costa Rica

The Sound of Death

On the Khakoo beach, he put the hat on his eyes and lay down. His muscular arms were pretty suntanned and their color was turning to black. Although he was tired of the smell of the sand and the sea, he always liked to lie down facing the sky so a thin layer of sea penetrated the space between him and the beach. Especially when he opened his eyes after a while and realized that he was a little farther than the spot that he had laid down in the beginning, without realizing it. However, he did that after he finished painting. In the past, when he did not know how to paint, he scribbled on his notebook and continued until exhausting all the ink in the pen, and he painted just to use up the ink and hear the scratching sound of the inkless pen. His painting was like scribbling and in fact, he learned that painting style through scribbling. The strokes that always depicted waves and rocks and showed the sea in a variety of moods like calm, semi-stormy and stormy conditions. The sound of the sea waves, which pacified the people and called everyone to silence, so they listen only to its monotonous and yet magical and hypnotic sound without thinking about other things, had another impact on Luis. This marvelous characteristic of the sea seemed more distinct to him. At those moments, his mind was more engaged than at any other time. He listened to the sound of the sea, mostly because he tried to imagine how it would sound when the sea was fully drained out. For example, he thought that if the sea was going to die, it would make a sound like the sound of the water draining down the toilet. He was actually very curious to know what the death itself could sound. The starting point of the curiosity went back to two months ago, one day after his mother's death. His mother was dying and as if her pupils had stuck under the arch of her eyebrows, repeatedly said, "I hear it! I hear it!"

Luis was anxious and upset. He had held his mother's hand in one hand and with his other hand tried to keep her shaky head steady.

– "What sound? Mom? You hear the sound of what?"

"Death! The sound. . . of death. . ." replied the mother.

Luis adjusted his hat. A curly-hair little boy was approaching him, trying to avoid coming into contact with the sea waves. The sea was calm and the boy dared to go a long distance from the beach and move along a zigzag course between the beach and the sea. He almost succeeded but the last time when his excited laugh made Luis aware of his presence, he could not escape and the wave went up to his knees. As he reached Luis and was going to shake him awake as usual and say, 'At the office, Mr. Martin wants you back there', Luis said promptly without removing the hat from his face, "I will be there in a moment!"

When he got up to go to Martin's hut, the lad who was a few steps ahead of him, began to repeat playing with the waves on the way back in the same manner as he was doing when he came for Luis. Luis ran slowly and put the boy behind and when he entered the hut, he said to Martin, "I have told you time and again, this child will grow up someday and will spoil your life for all of the unfulfilled children plays."

A Country Called the World

Martin patted his hairy chest and said, "Well, now what is the problem?"

Luis replied as he took a bottle of beer out of the refrigerator, "The poor child is polite even during playing. By seeing him, one can easily understand so much politeness does not fit that tiny body that is nearly bursting by so much excitement and energy."

Luis was the best and most skilled tour leader in Martin's company and Martin loved him more than his own child. He wished that someday his child grow strong and mighty like him. Therefore, unlike other tour leaders, he treated him very friendly and allowed him to do as he wanted. Martin insisted that people call his wooden hut *The Company*. The only person who helped him in his hut was his son and apparently, his most important duty was to inform Luis when Martin needed him.

Shortly after Luis's arrival, a young and pretty woman came out of the room dressed in white and got out of the hut after eyeing Martin coyly. Martin was waiting for Luis to finish the bottle in one gulp as usual, and said sarcastically, "Do you like to be a teacher? I am serious. I can ask my friends to find a teaching job for you! A teacher of ethics!"

Disregarding him, Luis began to drink the beer with a straw.

"Gentleman! You do not chug the bottle anymore! Observed Martin.

Shortly afterward when the beer was almost finished, Luis said, "Listen!"

Both heard the sound of the emptying bottle. It sounded like a gurgle.

Luis said, "How do you think the sea would sound when it is near the end?"

Martin, "The sun has fried your brain!"

Luis, "How do you think a flower would sound if its withering had a sound?"

Martin hit his own forehead hard and said, "You have really lost your mind! Get ready, the tourists are coming."

Luis, "Have you noticed that the humans gurgle at the time of death too? Like the sound of the beer in a bottle that finishes in a straw."

He approached Martin with a serious face.

Martin, "You are scaring me!"

He backed up with each step that Luis took toward him until he finally hit the wall and could not retreat farther. Luis raised the bottle and held it before Martin so he could catch the bottle from him. Martin took the bottle and Luis said, "I am always ready!"

Martin was really scared.

The tourists were a few young Scottish girls and boys who had just graduated in the field of philosophy. Luis paid more attention to them relative to the previous tourists and wanted to talk to them about the subject that had occupied his mind for a long time. So, when they were tired of walking around and followed their tour leader to their camp which was close to a nice سودا, Luis said, "Does anyone know what death sounds like? I mean, if the death was supposed to have a sound, how could it be?"

A boy who was the most talkative person among the crowd and always made his friends laugh and feel good, replied immediately, "Dude! Cut it out! We already have to deal with a lot of philosophical problems with life and death! We came here to stay away from those debates for a while."

Luis raised his hands as a sign of surrender and did not say anything.

When he took them to the camp and was on the way back, a redhead freckled girl went to meet him and said in Spanish, "Can you hear the sound of catching a cold, cancer, cholera, or the sound of sadness, happiness, and fear?"

Luis, indifferent to the good accent of the red-haired girl, shook his head no.

The girl said, "Death has no sound either."

"But if it had, how would it sound," said Luis.

The girl smiled and said, "Will you come to Afin De Barro with us tomorrow?"

"There is my colleague over there who will guide you," said Luis, and said goodbye to the girl with a smile and went away.

After he arrived home, he picked up the pen and opened the booklet. The booklet was full and the pen ink was nearly consumed. There was a small blank space at the top of one of the pages, and Luis, after realizing that if he kept his pen on the paper, its ink would drain out in a short while, began to doodle spirals, starting from the top of the page's blank area. The pen ink's color became lighter and lighter. Next, while being light colored, it finished in a trail of several vivid dots; just like a dying human being who at the last moments of his life, passes out and comes around several times. He had heard the sound of the draining pen quite a few times, but the sound always seemed fresh to him. Perhaps he never got tired of it because the pen was the only thing that he could easily hear the sound of its death. All of a sudden, he thought, 'Maybe based on the sound of the death of a creature whose sound of death I have never heard, I will discover the sound of the death itself."

After a while, he was granted leave and thus, he began to search. After staying awake for two days and nights in the room, in the silence that surrounded him thanks to sealing all the cracks and with great care, he heard the sound of the withering of the jasmine flower under the yellow light of the 100 Watt light bulb. The flower stem emitted a faint sigh when it died. Perhaps Luis imagined the sound of withering as such because he was imprisoned in the room for two days and he did not like his efforts turn out fruitless.

– "A sound like a little girl's moan!"

While he was deep in thought, he whispered that phrase and wrote it in the booklet. He did not notice the fact that he had imprisoned himself in the room for two days without food, water and rest. He continued to write, "Maybe a little weaker than the wince of a little girl after falling down. More like the sound of paper burning in the fire. No! A little fainter!" and after more concentration, he wrote again, "Or similar to the sound of a drying stream when the sun suddenly gets close to it! Like the sound of a shot bird that is certain it will not see the newly hatched chickens that are waiting for her."

He looked at what he had written up to that moment.

- "How poetic!" He said under his breath.

He unconsciously continued to write about what he had heard, and finally decided to send what he had written to the redhead girl. He continued to write excitedly for a few hours and after he likened the sound of the death of what he had heard recently to the sound of the death of things that he had heard and not heard before that time, he got up to go out of the room and immediately visit the redhead girl. But he felt giddy and fell to the floor on his side. A sound, like the sound of the wind, echoed in his ears. He fumbled around for the pen and paper that were at a little distance from him. But the pen ink was consumed and he could not immediately put down what he was hearing. Then he heard a faint moaning sound from his own throat, and finally, regretful of what he was hearing was the sound of his own death and not the sound of the death itself, passed away with an unanswered question whose answer was like all the answers that he knew, but none of them nonetheless.

A Country Called the World

A Country Called the World

Japan

The Wrong Prescription

Eleven months ago, Kazoku noticed that no one else was going to support her in life and went into isolation for some time. In those days, she put down all the hardships that she had endured in life on paper, so that every day – especially in tough circumstances –remind to herself by reading them that she was a diehard and also that she regretted to undergo ordeals in life for all kinds of reasons, but the hardships did not usher in any output and achievement for her and she did not attain a better standing.

Not that she had become cruel or frustrated, but she was insensitive to many incidents. For example, famine, flood, earthquake, and especially war and bloodshed among the people did not hurt her soul.

She thought to herself, 'My discomfort is to no avail. As long as there are ignorance, narcissism and a sense of supremacy, slaughter, murder, plunder, famine and war naturally comes to men.'

Even in last month when she was awarded the prize for the young Japanese poet of the year, she went to the podium in cool blood and said to all of the hundreds of the audience consisting of professional and amateur scholars and poets, families, and radio listeners, "I did my best. I used the words as much as I could, according to my power and taste and intellect and put down the poem. So, it is natural that the judges think my poetry is the best poetry of the year."

A Country Called the World

In the evening, Kazoku noticed the pages 106 to 112 of the book were blank and a part of the story was missed in print by mistake, so she closed the book and got out of the house. It was warmer outside, and the shops were usually open round the clock. Kazoku's home in Arakawa was very close to the Sumida River and she spent most of her time near the river, walking on the bridge.

She carefully examined the people's faces when they passed next to her. She was delighted to see a variety of emotions. Some were happy, some upset and depressed, some anxious, and some were proud.

— "How good is it that the people are not always happy, sad, angry, arrogant, depressed, or intoxicated, and what is better is that all human beings are not supposed to be happy or sad at the same time. However, it would not be all that bad either! Everyone would be simultaneously either sad or happy at any time. But it would be a boring world if they were supposed to be happy or sad at all times. Because the always-happy mankind would think it would not need any progress, and the always-sad mankind would think there would be no progress. Or, how would the world look like if emotions corresponded to the days of the week? All of the people would be happy on Sundays, sad on Mondays, proud on Tuesdays, depressed on Wednesdays, angry on Thursdays, and casual on Fridays. But no! It would not be a nice world. If the world was supposed to be as such from the next week, then it would be likely that the human race would go extinct from loneliness, suicide, and murder before reaching the second or third Tuesday, Wednesday and Thursday."

A Country Called the World

Kazoku's heart was full of joy by having the capability to think about those matters as such and she smiled at the joggers who quickly passed by.

From the perspective of the masses, a girl who, at the height of her youth and beauty and health, spent her time walking or sitting and thinking all by herself seemed to have suffered posttraumatic stress disorder, or for whatever reason, had lost the control over her life. Kazoku was well aware of this matter, and knew that the people were willing to endure a variety of sufferings but cannot take being alone and most of them even feared loneliness more than death,

– "Those who claim to have no fear of death are those who have lost one or more of their loved ones and thus, in the afterlife they are not alone since they know someone who has died before them."

Of course, pleasures, like narrating a marvelous adventure for a good friend, having fun, traveling, and talking to him, could not be underestimated but Kazoku was not the type of the person to spend time with anyone, especially friends, just because of fear of loneliness.

– "People who fear loneliness are dreadful human beings."

Kazoku never escaped loneliness because she always dealt with the respectful person that she herself was. A calm, purposeful and benevolent person.

A bit later she glanced at her wristwatch and walked in the same direction that she always walked and looked for a mark that she had put on the bridge's concrete guardrail with a piece of chalk two weeks ago. The mark was almost in the middle of the bridge. She stood near the mark for a few moments and glanced at her wristwatch again. It was 8,10 PM when Kazoku saw a young man with a white shirt (unbuttoned with the sleeves folded up to the elbow) and black pants was running toward her. The man waved and said a few steps before reaching Kazoku, "Hello!"

He bent down and hugged his knees and panted. He spat a piece of long laughter out of his throat and stammered, "You see! Obviously, I am alive!" and went on, "You stay here. . . I will be right back."

Kazoku watched the man as he went away and returned with two bottles of beer. The man said, "Here you are," as he wiped the sweat off a forehead that connected his sparse hair to his excited face.

Kazuku took the bottle and said, "Thanks."

Man, "Well, well, well! You talk first. What changes have you made to your life during these two weeks?"

Kazoku, "I am going to change my job this week. I want to be a swim coach. I am glad to see you happy. You have changed a lot!"

The man turned arrogantly and looked at the river for a few moments and said, "I want to jump and fly!"

Kazoku laughed and said, "What a change! In the past, you wanted to jump to your death. Now you want to jump to fly!"

The man smiled, took out a paper from a pocket and showed it to Kazoku, "Look! It's not too much, but it is very painful."

Kazoku stared at the man with a smile and an admiring eye and took the paper from him. A moment later, she wondered, "Why did you write the hardships before birth that your father and mother had endured when they were young?! And the hardships that you could not perceive because you were a small child! And also the hardships that your father and mother suffered when they had not yet met!"

The man replied with a self–righteous face, "However, the mistakes and ignorance of my parents when they were not yet married and did not know each other, strongly influenced the rise of problems and disputes between them when they married and their differences and problems contributed to the rise of the problems that I encountered later. My harsh life is rooted in the past. "

Kazoku, "You mean you two are going to blame your father and mother?"

Man, "Of course not. I am saying it did play a part. I am not saying they alone are the guilty ones."

He took a sip and put the bottle on the edge of the guardrail. After a little pause, he looked at the gray cobblestone and with a calm and sad tone, said under his breath, "But why did you ask me to write on the paper all the hardships and torments I got through in my life."

Kazoku heard his voice and said, "I thought you have figured that out."

Man, "To give up suicide?"

Kazoku, "Yes."

Man, "Do not you think that I only postponed the suicide?"

When he saw Kazoku's silence, he stared down at the river as he had been doing on many occasions in the last two weeks.

A Country Called the World

"So, why did not you take action over the past two weeks?" asked Kazoku.

The man kept looking at the river.

Kazoku said triumphantly, "Because you still love life deep in your heart."

The man said, "Maybe because I wanted to live a little bit in these two weeks," and rested his elbow on the bridge guardrail and looked at Kazoku, "Because in the last two weeks I spent my life as carelessly as I wished. I ate, slept, and had fun. Totally oblivious to the fact that I have a wife and a son! Goddamn both of them. After writing all the misfortunes that existed and continue to exist, I realized that I had to end my life much sooner, long ago. Perhaps my parents should have ended their lives before my birth so that we would not suffer this much torment and suffering. Hardships and sufferings made me abhor life. Because they repeat continuously and make my life predictable. Like some of the very prosperous people who after having all pleasures on earth, got bored of life," he continued with a sad smile, "Thank you for helping me to feel my misery as deep as possible!"

Kazoku realized that her prescription did no good to the man. She threw her bottle into a trash can and walked toward home. When the man saw Kazoku left him regardless of the possibility of an imminent horrible incident lurking around, he asked, "Do you see? Do you see a reason for me to go on living?"

Kazoku walked away without an answer. The man grabbed the bridge rod railing and abruptly screamed, "I am scared!"

A Country Called the World

Kazoku stopped. The passersby chattered and looked with surprise at the man's anxious and crying face and the girl who stood behind him a few feet away.

The man said, "I am fed up with this life and I fear suicide as well . . ." then he sat down on the same spot and rested his head on the guardrail and whispered, "I did not have the opportunity for trial and error and do not know what is my purpose in life, so I cannot go on . . ."

Kazoku returned home without glancing back.

Her parents had not yet returned from the trip. Kazoku switched on the lights and went to her room and sat down on the bed. A deep feeling of sin ran down her spine. She patted herself sympathetically and tried to look normal.

But the sound of a siren from afar induced heart palpitation, and her eyes, which had calmly and innocently started to the left just a moment ago, suddenly began to roll with fear. As the sound of the ambulance and the fire engine sirens grew louder, she immediately got up and looked out of the room's window. She stuck her head out as much as possible and as long as it was possible, tracked the path of the ambulance and the fire brigade. The vehicles went out of her field of view. Kazoku went to the kitchen window. From there, she could have a better view of the outside. A large crowd had gathered at the spot that Kazoku was standing a few minutes ago and were looking down.

Kazoku tried really hard to take it as normal but she could not help it and erupt in tears. A little later, she pulled out of the drawer the paper that she used to read its text every day after waking up and tore it to pieces.

A Country Called the World

A Country Called the World

Czech Republic

This Very Life

After Peter, Friedrich, Thomas, and Alan failed to join the Czech Republic's national boat team, they desperately decided to totally abandon this sport and fake insanity and live like crazy for the rest of their lives. So, according to the plan they had, they carried the boat and paddles to a corner of Thomas grandfather's farm to draw a lot to pick someone among themselves to set fire to them. Thomas volunteered to strike the match and in the blink of an eye, a fire with two meters' height, with red, orange, green and blue colors, lit up the corner of the farm up to a large radius. The cold January night's heart of the darkness melted by the tears of the four young men sitting next to the fire. From the moment of setting fire to the boat to its turning to charcoal, without exception, every one of the four men reviewed their sporting activities in their minds in full detail and if it was not for the sound of the grandfather's shotgun firing into the air, most probably they would have been sitting near the charcoal until the next morning. The grandfather pulled a long hose out of the barn and after attaching it to the water tap which was not far from the fire, went toward the young men.

When he was close enough to see their frightened faces, he said, "I was hoping at least you would not be one of those people who come to themselves with gunfire!"

He took Thomas's hand and helped him to stand up, and Thomas grabbed Friedrich's hand and Friedrich grabbed Peter's hand, but no one could help Alan off the ground by lending him a hand. Alan was sicker than to be able to take away his eyes from the paddles and the boat's charred remains which flickered on and off like a siren light. Finally, the grandfather picked him up by the armpit and sent them back to his house. Alan walked there by leaning on Peter.

– "Thomas, turn on the tap on your way."

The grandfather returned home after making sure there was no fire or hot charcoal left behind. When he arrived home, he saw Thomas filling his friend's glasses and thought to himself that it would be best to leave them alone.

Thomas, with the tone of a commander who was going to refresh the morale of the defeated and tired soldiers, said, "Let go of the sorrow. As we planned, for four nights, we first fake insanity in the presence of each other and afterward we will act like crazy everywhere. We can go to my house right now, which does not matter since my grandfather will not be back soon. Even if he returns, we will go to another room."

Thomas paused a bit and, knowing that his friends were waiting for him to talk first and also knew that if he was going to do it later, it was more likely that the friends might refrain from the decision they have made, popped his eyes and said with faked cheerfulness, "Gentlemen! I am going to recruit a boat team using four storks. I will be their coach. A strong team that will win all championship prizes every year."

In the end, he pounded the table hard with his fist and started to move an imaginary paddle in the air.

Except for Alan, the other friends who seemed to be somewhat motivated nodded as a sign of approval and welcomed

A Country Called the World

Thomas's words. Friedrich stared at a corner and while shaking his hands as if touched by a hot surface, said with a thin and feminine voice, "I will set up a boat and a paddle plant too. I will manufacture the best boats and paddles for Thomas!"

The friends nodded in agreement again.

Peter opened his arms, got up and walked around the table like a plane and said, "I will be the sponsor of Thomas's team!"

All looked at Alan. After a while, when he felt the weight of his friends' heavy gaze on him, he said unhappily, "Well, I will marry my girlfriend, we will make babies. Four storks. Then, I will send my storks off to Thomas's team that is well equipped. The only problem is that you must take your time to set up the plant or for coaching and sponsorship jobs till my storks grow up."

All laughed madly and after downing a couple of shots, the friends talked about their future plans with laughter. The hovercraft design of the boat, as well as materials that according to Friedrich, will be used instead of fiberglass in the construction of the boat to make it a thousand times lighter than other boats, a team with Thomas as the coach that thanks to professional members and a wealthy sponsor will win the prizes for years to come. Alan's children, who will be very strong and professional according to him, and another cheesy talk that went on till dawn.

The next night, everyone gathered in Friedrich's house the same way they did on the previous night.

Friedrich said, "I think it would be better to switch my place with Alan."

A Country Called the World

Alan, oblivious to his hint, got up and changed his place with Friedrich. Friedrich sat down on Alan's chair on the other side of the table and Alan sat on his chair. Alan seemed more upset than the previous night, and among the friends, he was the only one who spoke gibberish without faking anything, so he said, "Yes. I myself feel I am not ready to marry my girlfriend."

He looked at his dumb and foolish friends and patted his shaved head up and down in uncertainty and bewilderment. The landlord uttered rubbish and the rest elaborated on that with their own nonsense.

Friedrich was still waving his hands, staring at the floor with narrowed eyelids. After a few seconds, he said happily, "I will marry her! But *you* father her child. I just want to manufacture the boat and the paddle and it does not matter to me who are the team members. But since you insist that the team members should be chosen to your liking, we will set up the team using your four kids."

Thomas and Peter nodded in agreement with Friedrich's words. It was at the tip of Alan's tongue to say, 'You already have a girlfriend!'; but he did not say it and laughed out loud. Then Thomas, like a toddler who had wetted his diapers, walked aside with a wide gait and slow pace and called them to himself. They went to Thomas, Peter like a plane, Friedrich like a hopping Gorilla, and finally, a reluctant Alan with a ridiculous smile. The friends piled up their hands as a sign of unity and solidarity and threw up their arms on the count of one; two, three and each said something different, "Tomatoes. Sperm. Scarecrow. Victory." The *Victory* came out of Alan's mouth. In the past, the friends habitually shouted that in unison before each race.

A Country Called the World

Friedrich filled the glasses and the friends talked again about their future plans with the difference this time, they described the finer detail of the plans. The fiddle-faddle and ridiculous behavior! Just like crazy people!

The next night, at Peter's house, the landlord walked up and down the house with his hands behind his back and said, "It is not fair! But we can still shine. No! We gave up too soon!" he uncorked the whiskey bottle, "We will go on! Thomas should be both the coach and the teammate. I and Friedrich will also both serve our new posts and as teammates."

Friedrich and Thomas nodded in agreement.

"Any place for me in the team?" joked Alan.

Peter said, "Oh, I am sorry Alan. We will set up a team of three. We do not need you."

The friends confirmed Peter's words again and began having fun and debauchery after kicking Alan out of the house. Alan was certain that his friends were crazy. So, he walked home with increasing frustration.

In the last night, they all gathered at Alan's house. The friends crazily pushed the doorbell and pounded on the door and then entered the house with their role-playing routine.

Alan knew that his friends would accept any claptrap that he may suggest, "What is your opinion about setting up a team consisting of one calf and three turtles?"

The friends nodded in agreement and welcomed his offer.

"We must switch our places, Friedrich," said Alan.

Friedrich got up from his chair and sat down on his chair.

A Country Called the World

Alan also got up, walked slowly toward the kitchen and asked, "What is your opinion about setting up a team of three?"

Friends agreed with Alan, as they climbed on the table and waited for him to fetch the whiskey. Contrary to the previous nights that after getting drunk, they sat down on the table in a row and moved their imaginary paddles, on that night they began the routine before Alan returned with the glasses. Alan could imagine them in the same situation in a lunatic asylum. He was very angry with the foolish decision they had taken. He walked quickly as he changed his destination from the kitchen to the bedroom. After a few seconds, he turned to his friends carrying a pistol and shouted, "What do you think about that I am going to shoot you all?"

Everyone rose from their places and looked at Alan with fear.

Alan, with shaky hands and spraying saliva, was thrown out of his mouth, said, "Why do we have to fake madness?"

Friedrich, "We have no other choice, do we? We can no longer live like ordinary people."

"We could have made it," Alan shouted, "We had the chance not to be fired from the team and find our way to the national team. You did not take it seriously."

Thomas, "You know that the coach did not like us."

Alan, "Bad coach, poor facilities, old boat all are your preposterous excuses."

Then, as he pointed the gun toward his friends in turns, asked, "Between death and living like crazy, which one do you choose?"

A Country Called the World

Everyone was silent and looked at Alan. Alan swore he would kill them if they did not answer.

Alan, "Answer me you bastards! Which one do you choose between death and living like crazy?"

Thomas said calmly, "This very life."

Alan, "I did not hear you!"

Thomas, "I said this very life!"

***

Alan was using a hypothetical paddle in the presence of the inspector and the police, as well as in the court, and repeatedly said, "I have children who will be great boatmen someday, provided that I have a reasonable coach and sponsor and facilities."

He did not believe his friends had died. He did not believe that he had committed homicide.

Eight months after his detention at the madhouse, one day that he was talking to himself as usual and repeated his plans loudly, a patient who had just entered the lunatic asylum asked him, "Have you committed murder?"

Alan nodded as he talked to himself.

A Country Called the World

A Country Called the World

Cameroon

The Photographer

On May 22, Alice, the only child of Mr. and Mrs. Simo, turned five and got a Polaroid photographic camera as a birthday present from her parents. In fact, the gift was presented by the owner of the lumber factory where Mr. Simo worked. Once, when Mr. Simo's daughter and wife went to the factory, the factory owner saw from the window of his room that Alice was finger framing her hands and focused the frame every few seconds on a different subject, and after a pause and saying "Chick, Chick", moves to another subject in the same way again. Sometimes, when the workers saw Alice's hands, they smiled and stroke poses so their pictures look good. Alice had many photos. Before they buy her a camera, she had a lot of pictures of her smiling parents, her mother's sad face, her father's work clothes, an aged couple walking on the sidewalk, a boy falling down in the street and other subjects. Of all the photos that she had stored in the memory using her finger frame, she most loved the photos of the laughing people, especially her parents.

On the birthday night, Alice's only aunt along with two orphan newborn babies who she had recently adopted came from the beautiful city of Buea to Mr. Simo's house. The first photograph taken with Alice's camera was her own image blowing out the candles on the cake. She looked into the lens and the photo was taken by the father.

A Country Called the World

"The photo must be shaken a few times. Like this. Aha!" said the father.

With surprise and joy, Alice watched her photo slowly appearing. She took a lot of photos on her birthday night and while she was happily going around taking photos of all the birthday moments, she realized that the camera took a shot of one of the best moments but did not discharge it for development. The mother had already advised her not to take photos sparingly and keep the camera tape rolling for special moments but the father downplayed it by saying 'All the birthday moments are beautiful and special!' and allowed her daughter to take pictures whenever she wanted to.

The father, as he was taking a spoonful of cake to the mother and the mother with an open mouth, found out that the camera film had finished.

To keep Alice happy, the father said, "Darling, you take the photos. I will develop them later."

Alice took the photos with a blank camera. On the next day, when she put the pictures together on the floor of her room with her mother, she knew that the last image, at the time of which the camera tape was exhausted and did not record it, turned out to be the best of them all.

The mother pointed to a photo and said, "Look at this photo! You look so cute!"

But Alice wanted to see the last photo as soon as possible. They were checking the pictures when the phone rang. Alice thought that up to that moment, she had no photos of her parents on the phone. Therefore, she took a shot of the mother with the blank camera so her father could develop it later. The mother was upset after she put down the handset. She took Alice to the yard without saying a word put her shoes on and they went out of the house. Alice, with the camera swinging on her neck, walked quickly lest her mother thinks she moved slowly because of the camera's weight and suddenly remove the camera from her neck and throw it away.

When they arrived at the factory, the father had been taken to the hospital. The factory manager took them to his office.

– "Calm down! Do not cry, it is not good for your daughter. Believe me, nothing has happened and he will be discharged soon."

The mother cried, "His coworkers said the timber fell on his chest," and embraced her daughter as if she was going to calm down her child and console her. Mrs. Simo and her daughter sat at the office of the manager for a short time and then went to the hospital. Three of Mr. Simo's ribs were broken and his left knee and skull were severely damaged. He was lying unconscious on the hospital bed and did not notice the sound of his wife crying. An hour after their arrival at the hospital, a young physician went to Mrs. Simo and said, "He will live a hard life even if he survives."

The next day, when Mr. Simo regained consciousness, he said after muttering delirium, "Alice ..."

Mrs. Simo smiled and said, "We will be going home soon," and brought Alice, who was taking pictures with the blank camera from all corners of the hospital, to her husband so he could caress Alice's face with his feeble hand.

Mr. Simo died five days later. After the burial of her husband, Mrs. Simo went to the manager's office at the factory to cash Mr. Simo's little payment from him.

The factory manager said, "I do not owe him much," then he sat down opposite to Alice, looked at the camera, and said, "My dear! I love the photographic camera. Do you like the camera too?"

Mrs. Simo pushed Alice's hair off her face and said, "Alice loves photography." The chairman removed the camera from Alice's neck and said, "Do not hang the camera on your neck. It is too heavy for your delicate neck."

He put the camera in front of his eyes and took a picture of Mrs. Simo and after a few moments of waiting, said, "No way! The camera tape is finished."

Mrs. Simo said with embarrassment, "It has been a long time since there is no tape in it."

The factory chairman pulled out his own camera's tape and said, "One cannot take pictures without a tape. A camera without tape is like a man without income. Totally useless."

As soon as he was going to put the tape on Alice's camera, Mrs. Simon stopped him.

The factory chairman returned the camera to Alice and said, "Go take a few shots to see how good a photographer are you!"

Alice was descending slowly from the iron stairs. She turned for a moment to see her mother staring ahead and the factory manager closing the door to his room. She immediately took a shot with her camera. Again, she took another shot of the factory manager pulling the room's curtains and also her mother who was putting her bag on his table when she stepped down the stairs. A few moments later, the curtains blocked Alice's line of sight. So, she went to the workers to take photos of them, but suddenly she saw her mother rushing down from the manager's room. To record that scene, there was no need for the camera to be equipped with tape or to form a finger frame. The frightened face of the chairman rolling and falling down the stairs with a knife in his stomach was impressed in Alice's mind forever.

The factory manager, repeatedly and even before Mr. Simo was injured, made advances to Mrs. Simo quite a few times. So, Mrs. Simo was right to think that the factory manager had set up a plot to eliminate Mr. Simo to achieve his end that way.

Sixteen years later, when Mrs. Simo was released, she saw the young Alice and her sister and decided to tell them, 'Forgive me that I was not at your side at the best moments of your life,' but Alice did not say a word from the prison's gateway to the front of the house and did not allow her mother to say anything either.

– "Just look! Look at everything that is around."

Mrs. Simo had met Alice may times in prison when she came to visit her, but it was out of the jail that she noticed her daughter had grown up, and what caught her eyes most of all was this matter, not seeing the birds and the sky and the people, etc., that Alice expected by walking slowly, her mother could enjoy watching such scenes.

For a long time, Mrs. Simo was amusing herself with the photos that Alice brought her every now and then. Beautiful photos of her sister and two children, natural landscapes, laughing faces, gourmet food, entertainment centers, animals, etc. On her last day in prison, when Alice went to see her, she did not take any photos with her.

"What was the best photo you ever saw?" she asked her.

The mother pointed to the eleven bags of photos in her cell and said, "They are all beautiful to me. But what is your take?"

Alice held her mother's face between her two hands and as she examined her deep-set eyes and weary face, said, "The photo in which my mom did not allow herself to be abused was the best photo I have ever seen."

A Country Called the World

The United Kingdom

Escape from the Claws of Science

Tom, a twenty-year-old boy with no academic education unlike his educated siblings, in response to his friend George who asked him on his way home back from the work that, 'What do you want from life?' said, 'I wish I was the author of Hamlet. I had built the Manchester Spinning Factory. I had discovered Earth gravity. Darwin's achievements were mine."

George, "No. I did not ask whose shoes you would like to be. Now! What do you want from life now?"

Tom, "Nothing."

George, "You mean you want to work at the print shop for the rest of your life? Hear the machinery noise, throw up by the smell of paper and oil, move hundreds of book boxes, not allowed to speak, and waste your days on this lousy job?"

Tom smiled and said, "Yes. Believe me, my friend, it is all that we measure up to and we cannot change it for better."

George stopped for a moment and anxiously looked at his friend. Again, he met his pace and said, "I have a suggestion."

Tom, "Suggestions are good to improve the situation and solve the problem. I neither want my situation to improve, nor do I have any problems."

George, "I need your help."

Tom laughed hard and said, "You need no suggestion to ask for help! Comrade!"

A Country Called the World

George, "Once again, works instead of me for two more months during the day so that I can study well and get ready to go to college."

Tom, "You deleted the second part of the sentence!"

George, "You are really smart, comrade! As I said before, after I am able to continue to study and attain a better position, I will help you to improve your situation too. If you like it, of course."

Tom, "I would rather only help you and do not accept the offer. By the way! This is the fifth time you attempt to go to college?!"

George, "The fourth time! Ha, ha."

Ten years after George graduated from the high school with difficulty and low scores, he applied once to enter the Faculty of Medicine and twice to enter the Faculty of English Language and Literature and was rejected with the lowest scores. He made friends with Tom at a later time after applying for the examinations required to enter the college.

Unlike Tom's empty house, George had a large library in his house surrounded by the poetry of T. S. Elliot and William Blake and other masters which were all over the place, from the entrance to the walls and the fridge and above the mirror, and even in his son's room. After he departed from his pessimistic friend and arrived home, he casually hugged his son, who rushed to him enthusiastically, and kissed him. He dined hastily and, like the other times that he had driven his wife up the wall by trying to enter the college, asked her to cope with him again and sweat it. Next, under the sorrowful gaze of his wife with a frozen spoon between her plate and her mouth, went to their small room, sat on a chair, and covered his ears and oblivious to objections to the rights of the wife began to study for the tests.

A Country Called the World

He kept a bottle of water at hand and scanned the relevant books line by line and every few minutes when his mind was overwhelmed, he drank the water and stretched the skin on the side of his forehead, as if trying to increase his brain's capacity and volume.

For several nights in a row, a lot of noise was heard from the large and beautiful mansion of Mr. & Mrs. Krach on Park Lane Street. Tom walked to his room and said, "Father! Mother! I want to be a worker. Go in the morning and come back in the evening, live normally, do not ask for more, do not have intellectual and educated friends, my brain would not have the capacity to learn science, do not explore and discover, when I see a nice landscape I would not be going to be inspired, be anxious by the possibility of not meeting the ends, and live at the lowest social class."

He rolled up his sleeves, kicked open the door to the room, and went in. The father had stood with hands on his waist and looked at his wife with amazement and discomfort, and Mrs. Krach, engulfed in grief, looked alternately at the room's door and her husband's face. A bit later, Tom stepped out of the room and took his dish from the table, which was perfectly arranged for dinner.

– "I am both angry and pissed off! Because the rent of the house that I am going to stay in is just a little lower than my income. That means I cannot save anymore!"

By saying that, he went to his room and shut the door.

In the middle of the night, when Tom was in a deep sleep and even the intense wind that had begun to blow for a while could not wake him up; he had a bad nightmare and woke up. He was not sleepy anymore. He held his head firmly between his two hands and desperately tried to stop thinking. Topics like the speed of a meteorite, formation of black holes, volume of supernovas, speed of light, movement of planets and the asteroids, number of galaxies, probability of the existence of other worlds, possibility of living on another planet, as well as the most complex physics and mathematics problems invaded his mind.

***

Tom helped his friend as expected, but George did not succeed again. George never realized that Tom was a very clever and talented boy so much that anytime he would like to, he could study at the best university in the field of astronomy. So, the day after getting the test result, he did not expect to hear encouraging and nice words from him. Because during the time he had been friends with him, he had realized that Tom was an easy going and miserable man.

Tom, "I do not see any reason to worry."

George, "*I* did not pass it. So, *you* should not be upset. You were right. We cannot make progress."

Tom, "We have arrived at my home. Come in, and I have a suggestion!"

George, "Do you live in White chapel too?!"

Tom, "Yes, it is a couple of days that I moved here."

Tom's house had thirty-three stairs leading up to the fifth floor. The walls of the corridor were freshly painted and the stairs were not guarded. The house was overtly empty because George was certain that Tom's monthly wage was not enough to fill the fridge and buy a new bed and furniture and a better door instead of the thin wooden door which could be easily opened even when locked.

Tom, "You see; this is my life. I do not know about you, but I live like this. I mean I have no choice. Do you want to get educated?"

George, "I do not know. I am afraid I will continue to mess it up again. I could not save any money since I did not work for the last two months. It was a loss."

Tom smiled and went to the window to pull the curtain aside. The evening light added to the sad atmosphere of the house.

George asked Tom, "You mean you are not going to apply for the college again?"

George, "No. I like to continue my life as it is then to incur loss time and again."

By seeing his friend's dirty life, who seemed grateful though, and repeatedly reviewing his past experiences that every time he wanted to make some progress, he regressed a few steps back from the start point, he felt he was deeply interested in his life and what he was. So, he said regretfully, "How stupid I was to think I had to study to enjoy life."

"It is never too late to appreciate life," said Tom, confident that George would never return to science again, "My suggestion is to teach your child to avoid study, live like you, and enjoy it."

A Country Called the World

A Country Called the World

Denmark

Black

When Emily heard her father's voice exclaiming happily, 'Come see what I hunted!', immediately went down the stairs and saw his father, Christine IV, was holding up a large bird upside down with an arrow protruding from one of its wings. The bird seemed alive and stirred. Emily looked at it for a while and then suddenly began to cry and attacked her father, "You should not have done this! You should not have done this!"

The queen came and hugged her daughter, covered her eyes, and said to her husband uncomfortable, "No need to shout it out! Everyone knows that you are a skilled hunter."

When the queen and his daughter went away, the king said to himself naively, "I just wanted you to see that I hit a bird in the air. Finally, I made it."

Maybe if his three other daughters, Caroline, Sophie, and Shaun, were in the palace at that moment, they would have felt sick like Emily.

***

Under the laws of the king, a child who reached the age of sixteen had to assume the administration of a part of the country, and instead of living with the family, had to live in a separate palace. It was two weeks before Caroline, the king's oldest daughter, had to go to her palace.

Caroline, "I miss home."

A Country Called the World

Sophie and Shaun, as they were combing her hair, said at the same time, "I miss you too." Their utterance of the same statement accidentally and simultaneously provoked them to pinch each other's cheeks.

Sophie, "You always pinch my cheeks hard!"

The mother, while holding the hands of the eldest daughter, laughed and looked at their white faces that turned red with the slightest touch and said, "You do not have to hurt yourselves," then she called one of the maids, "Where is Emily?"

The maid, who was panting due to descending the stairs, said, "She does not answer no matter how many times I call her."

Emily had placed the stool near the window and did not take her eyes off the shadow of a bird that had sat on the roof. She stretched out her arm to measure the size of the bird's shadow with the index finger and thumb. From that distance, the shadow of the bird was as thick as the fabric of her skirt. She was busy thinking, 'What could that bird be?' when her mother hugged her. As she found herself in the arms of her mother, who was kissing and caressing her as she carried her down the stairs, she showed her hand to her which had still preserved the size of the bird's shadow and asked, "Have you ever seen a bird this size?"

The mother pressed her firmly to her chest and said, "Oh, my dear!"

"I have!" said Emily.

Mother, "What you are showing is an ant, not a bird!"

She firmly kissed her face again, so much so that Emily had to push her back, both because she wanted to explain more to her and because her eye was really hurt.

A Country Called the World

She insisted as she was rubbing her eyes, "I said the truth. I saw it. A bird as tiny as this."

The mother went close to her daughters and held up Emily as if she was going to throw her and said, "Anyone needs a bird?! A little fascinating bird!"

Emily began laughing at her mother's jokes and tickling and opened her arm like the wings of a bird.

"I want it! Come here! You are my bird!" said Caroline.

Emily found herself in the arms of her sister who kissed her all over like her mother.

The next morning, when everyone was getting ready for the party, Emily saw the bird's shadow again out of the window. But this time, she was looking at it through Sophie's window. Sophie was about to comb her hair, but when she saw Emily sitting on the windowsill, got out of the room impatiently and joined her sisters, servants, and mother; because she had to stretch her arm too far to comb Emily's hair which embarrassed her. Again, Emily noticed the bird's shadow was very small. She could not imagine any wings, beak, tail, and feathers for a bird with such an infinitesimal size. She thought even its color should be black just because the shadow was black. A bit later, slowly and without drawing attention, she went down the stairs and entered their room. No! Again, the bird seemed very tiny. So, she went into Caroline's room. The bird's shadow was the size of a thumbnail. Emily, as she was looking at its size, said, "This bird is very small! I would easily lose it or gets crushed."

Then she went into her parents' room and as soon as she was going to climb up the bed to reach the window, the room-service maid saw her and said, "Little lady! Do not you know you should not enter someone's room without permission! Let's go, your mother called you a few times."

She took Emily's hand to take her out but Emily abruptly freed her hand and climbed up the bed and reached the window. The bird was gone. Emily surrendered to the maid and joined her family gathering.

Unlike her sisters who were having fun, laughing, and celebrating, she was constantly looking at the floor to hopefully see the bird. Everyone was having fun and no one noticed Emily.

The king was surrounded by the people and was shooting at a target which was at a great distance. All the arrows that left the bow hit the center of the target. The king loudly invited his cousins, who looked at him with envy, to a contest. None could beat him at shooting, fencing, and wrestling. So, it was not too surprising that the cousins sat with their mistresses at a corner in the shade like harmless vegetation and looked at him.

The king's family doctor also hinted at that with a laugh, "If I am going to pick an unknown plant, I would be a little anxious and cautious lest that plant is poisonous, but your cousins are even less harmless than plants!"

The celebration and dance party was in full swing and food and booze was abundant and the people were very happy about the fact that the feast and celebration could go on for quite a few days. The queen had sat next to a group of her friends and talked to them about literature and architecture. Caroline had also sat beside her mother and pretended that she was carefully listening to her, but in fact, her heart was beating with the prospect of having an intimate moment with the physician's son, her new crush. She was waiting for an opportunity to meet him again beside the Enchanting River. (They say that in the old days, a poet went to this river for inspiration and lost his mind by seeing its beauty. For this reason, people called it the Enchanting River.) At a corner, a bit farther than the people's joy and dancing, the children's play, the screeching laughter of women, and the chefs who were sweating abundantly; Emily saw the shadow of a few birds fleeing from her. She was bored and wanted to return to the palace as soon as possible to look at the bird's shadow from her parents' room. Although they were not far from the palace, she did not know the way.

The chief servant was walking among the chefs to make sure everything was alright. He was a jack of all trades, but cooking was his best skill. He noticed that someone was pulling his hand as he was talking to one of the cooks next to a bowl.

Emily, "I must go to the bathroom."

The servant took her to a corner, but Emily said, "No, I must go to my own bathroom. I am not comfortable here."

The servant gestured to the queen from afar that he was going to take Emily to the bathroom.

Emily, after faking the need for the bathroom, asked the servant to take her to her parents' room so that she could pick up her hairpin that she claimed she had dropped by the bed.

"But my dear, your hair is perfect," said the servant.

He patted Emily's head and picked her up to take her away but Emily began to cry, "I want my hairpin."

The servant had to take her to the room of the king and the queen. As a matter of fact, he was not reluctant to go to their room at all. He was eager to lie upon the bed of the king and the queen once and roll over like kids.

A Country Called the World

"You search that spot," said Emily and pointed to the right side of the bed and went to the left where the window was. She saw the servant was busy combing the floor to find the hairpin and climbed up the bed and reached the window. She saw the bird's shadow! Immediately, she took the right action. The bird's shadow seemed a bit larger than the previous times when Emily measured it.

– "No, it is not here, and here!"

The servant, oblivious to Emily who was sitting by the window, was lying on the bed and looked under the pillows searching for the hairpin. Emily came down the window and picked up her hairpin that she had dropped near the door before going to the party, and said, "I found it!"

The size of the hairpin was exactly the size of the bird's shadow. The size of two finger joints. She could easily imagine shape and appearance for a bird of that size. A jet black bird that could talk to Emily like humans.

At night, some of the people slept on the premises of the feast, and the others returned to their homes. When the king's family and servants returned to the palace, Emily was caressing the bird on her legs in the carriage. When they arrived at the palace and everyone went to their rooms, Emily noticed that she had closed the door before the bird could come in. So, she slowly opened the door just enough for the bird to sneak in. The bird entered the room. The candles were lit, but the bird's eyes could not be seen due to sheer blackness. It looked around for a while. Then, it saw Emily sitting on the bed, looking at it.

"Come here, beside me," said Emily.

The bird stepped closer to her.

A Country Called the World

Emily, "I call you *Black*!"

The bird said, "What the …? Oh, yeah, Black really fits me. What is *your* name?"

Before Emily could tell her name, Black said, "No, do not say a thing. I myself will find a name for you."

Emily put her hands under its head. She was eager to know what name Black would choose for her.

Black, "I know a beautiful blue-gray colored river. Like the color of your eyes, and there is a wheat field next to it, which doubles its beauty."

Emily showed her blond hair to Black.

"Yes, it is exactly the same color of your hair. The riverbed is also as white as your skin. They call this river the Enchanted River. I call you Enchanted!"

Emily, "What a nice name! Sometimes my mom calls me by this name."

Black, "Hey, do you teach me how to fly?"

Emily, "First, promises we will be friends forever. After that, I will teach you how to fly."

Black, "I promise I will never leave you if I learn to fly."

Therefore, Black and Emily made friends and wherever Emily went, she took Black with her. When eating, she pushed some of her food to the side, so Black could eat too. In the parties, she did not play with the kids of her age and was busy with Black. At night, she told it stories and rarely got out of her room. A few days later, she told one of the servants to make a nest for Black. The servant built several nests and demolished them, until finally; Black whispered in her ear as it sat on Emily's shoulder, "I like this nest."

Emily placed its nest beside her bed.

On the last day of the presence of the eldest sister in the palace, Emily was jumping up and down in her room like in the last few days, "Let's try again. Look at me carefully. Open your wings, jump and start to flap!"

Then, she jumped and shook her hands. Black jumped up and down the same way, but there was no improvement over the recent days.

Emily said, "Ok, let's try it another way. First, move your wings, and then jump. Like this."

Black raised from the floor a little bit and could fly for a few moments.

Emily said, "Aha, you flew! Let's try again."

At that moment, the mother entered her room, "Dear! Get ready to go!"

"I am teaching Black how to fly. You go yourself," said Emily.

The mother took her hand and said, "Let Black learn flight on its own," and led her down the stairs. Emily looked back. She saw Black flew a few steps with a little distance from the floor and came out of the room and landed again.

"You will eventually do it! I am right here," said Emily.

Black said happily, "I am flying!"

When the mother dressed Emily with the party outfit in the lobby, Emily had placed one of her hands on the mother's shoulder and was moving her legs to ease putting on her white velvet panties, and then she saw Black was flying near the railing of the corridor which connected her room to the four large halls.

Black flew with difficulty from the Emily room's doorway to the last hall with a little distance from the floor. It flew higher and comfortably on the way back from the last hall toward Emily's room. It flew without falling to the floor and began to fly up and down the palace. Emily was thrilled and looked at it with a smile.

When everyone was going out of the palace, Black noticed Emily's uptight complexion and said, "You go, I will catch up with you."

Emily waited a long time at the party but did not see Black, because it was a cloudy day. When the celebration ended, Emily immediately returned to her room, "Why did not you come?!"

"I came. But you did not see me," said Black, standing by the window under the candlelight.

Emily, "So I did not imagine it! You were actually sitting and speaking on my shoulder today! I heard your voice a few times."

Black, "Yes, I said 'I am here! I came! Enchanted!' a couple of times, but you did not hear it. I think your mind was occupied by your sister's yummy cake! Ha, ha."

Emily laughed and did not notice the presence of her mother.

Mother, "Do you want to sleep with me tonight?"

Emily, "I have to consult with Black."

Mother was surprised to see Emily asking the candle, "What is your opinion?" Then she looked at her uncomfortably and said,

"Did not you say we must knock when we go to each other's room?!"

"My darling, I knocked but you did not hear it," laid the mother, then she sat down and took Emily's hands, "Come sleep with me tonight."

"What's up?" asked the king, standing at the doorway.

The queen, without turning back to look behind her, said, "Mr. Hunter! Do you see what have you done!" and patted Emily's face.

"What did I do?" wondered the king.

The queen let go of Emily and pulled the king outside along with her, "This kid does not look fine at all! Why did not we take her malady seriously?! Everyone is playing, singing and dancing. She stares at a corner without talking to anyone and sometimes mumbles and laughs. What's more, when she eats, a tablespoon of food always remains uneaten on her plate. Look!"

She went back to Emily's room again and asked, "My dear, will you sleep with me tonight? In my room."

Emily felt threatened by her parents' small talk, and before her mother entered her room for the second time, said to Black, "If I go to their room, you come after me. I will open the door for you."

Then, without saying anything threw herself into the mother's arms.

Emily lay down on the bed between her father and mother, closed her eyes, and pretended to sleep, but waited for them to go to sleep so she could go and open the door for Black. It was dark all over and no candles were burning. Emily heard the Black's voice, "It's me! Look at the window."

When a thunderbolt illuminated the room, Emily saw black flapping its wings behind the window.

Emily, "When did you go out?"

Black, "Did not you hear it? Your father threw the cage out."

Emily, "I am sorry that I could not take care of you."

A teardrop rolled down her eye and added, "We are still friends. Is it not so?"

There were other thunder and lightning.

Black said, "We will be friends forever. You are my BFF. You taught me how to fly."

Emily, "But you left me."

Black, "I told you that I was in the cage. Your father threw it out. Do not worry. I will be back one day."

And with the next sound of thunder, Emily could not see Black anymore. No matter how many times she called it, there was no answer.

Mother, "Emily! Emily!"

The king got up and lit the candles. Emily looked at her family who were staring at her. After a few seconds, she said to the king, "Why did you throw the cage out!" and began to cry and buried her face in the pillow. The kids, who had just arrived there by the sound of ruckus, we are looking at their father.

King, "Your sister is not alright."

"Ok, kids. Go to your room," said the mother.

A Country Called the World

Sophie and Shaun immediately went down with the maid, but Caroline stayed there and embraced her sister.

The king sat beside the queen, caressed Emily, and said, "I am sorry."

The next day, all of the people gathered to escort Caroline on the way to her palace. That day was more or less cloudy, and Emily, as she dressed up with a sad face, decided to not to speak to anyone till she met Black again.

A Country Called the World

Afghanistan

The Last Drop of Credit

He quickly passed through the marketplace. He had reached a level of hunger that he felt nausea by seeing foodstuff. However, he had to get some food because weakness and distress would return to his body soon. A few steps farther than the market, he leaned on the wall and thought what other excuses he could find to purchase from his friend's shop on credit. He was close to the shop and on the other side of the market; his worn-out house was looking odd with a pale smoke of burning lean firewood coming out of the chimney. First, he had to go home because he needed a toilet. He tried hard to contain himself so he could go home after going to the shop but he could not help it. So, he passed through the market again and reached his home.

Even if a person who was not hungry came to his house, he would have easily realized that there was no food to eat and he did not need to go to the kitchen to find it out. Ahmad decided to overcome shyness and buy on credit from his friend for the umpteen times. The growl of his stomach encouraged him to put his decision into action. He pocketed a few leaves of mint left from the previous day's lunch to chew them when entering the shop and the bad smell of his mouth would not disturb the shopkeeper.

Since Ahmad was a kind and educated person, whenever he talked to the shopkeeper, his mind that was filled with knowledge and wisdom calmed down his friend and heartened him. The shopkeeper strongly needed Ahmad's words, because, in his opinion, Ahmad was the only one who had a different and interesting attitude about life. The fact that man can always progress and life is amazing and beautiful at all times, was some of the things that Ahmad talked about them with solid reasoning for his friend, who was suffering amongst illiterate, greedy and clueless people. That is why the shopkeeper always granted Ahmad's purchase on credit without any objection.

Of course, this time it was very improbable to purchase on credit since it was nine months that Ahmad had not paid back his debt to him. That is, all merchandise bought on credit during that period had root in a loan that he had taken from him nine months before that.

He stopped in front of the shop for a few moments and remembered how tolerant was his friend was. All of his notches on the wood were struck out[1] and there was no longer any credit left. During those nine months, his friend sold him on credit as long as he was confident that Ahmad would settle his debt. More or less, he allowed him to take away whatever he wanted. About a week ago when Ahmad purchased on credit, the shopkeeper opened his books and realized that he should no longer grant on-credit transactions because his educated friend might not be able to pay back his loan more than what he had already owed. Therefore, he did not write the debt related to that day in his accounts book and by that gesture, told him that he must be fair and settle his unwritten debt figure. Even two days later that Ahmad needed a little money, he lent him, not from his petty cash but the money in the charity collection box inside

---

[1] Notches made in a piece of wood in ancient times to remember one's purchases on credit.

the shop. Ahmad was a bit annoyed by the fact that his friend gave him money from the charity box but he thought that his situation did not differ much from the oppressed people, so he should not be upset.

It was noon and his friend did not have many customers. After his only customer left, Ahmad entered the shop with a cold, unobtrusive face. His friend was murmuring a Bazgl Badakhshi's[1] the song with a smiley face. When he saw Ahmad, he said to him, "Hello my friend, I missed you!"

He went to Ahmad and hugged him. He usually missed Ahmad if he was not around. On that day, he was really cheerful and happy.

Ahmad, "Yes, I missed you too. You look so happy!"

His friend opened the candy box in front of him, "My baby was born!" then he laughed and said, "You can eat this confectionery as much as you can!"

Ahmad put a piece of confectionery in his mouth and put another six pieces in a plastic bag to take home with him. He did not feel like eating confectionery and a piece or a box of it did no good to him. But anyway, that was a bargain. He wanted to eat a hamburger. He asked after putting the confectionery in his mouth, "Was it born today?"

"No, yesterday," said the shopkeeper, then he turned his head to look at the clock and said, "Half an hour afternoon! This boy is really absent-minded. I told him that I should go home early today but he did not care at all."

---

[1] A country music singer (1903-2010 A.D.).

A Country Called the World

Ahmad thought to himself that if he had one percent chance to still buy on credit from his friend, that chance would be zero if his friend's brother arrived. Because all of his tickets held by the shopkeeper's brother had been toasted too, and he could not get anything on credit from him at all.

So, he quickly said, "Can I take a pack of hamburgers? I have not eaten for a day."

He could get it on credit easier than he thought. Although the shopkeeper was delighted that his child was born, a little later, when in the weighing scale of his mind he put the unpleasant feeling of giving credit to Ahmad versus the happiness caused by the birth of his baby, he realized that the unpleasant feeling was heavier. So, as Ahmad seized the pack of hamburgers, he said with a serious face, "You do not bring its money and disturb me."

Ahmad glanced indifferently at the shopkeeper and said, "This time, I will definitely bring the money of this piece of merchandise."

He picked up the pack of hamburgers.

"No, you will not. I know you will not. Recently, you have been repeating the same thing as you take away the goods. But you did not bring it," said his friend.

Ahmed stared at his friend with a serious face and said, "Look! Look right into my eyes! I have never lied to anyone eye to eye. This time when I said I will bring it, I definitely will."

By saying that, he was certain that the shopkeeper would no longer protest. So, he boldly took another pack of hamburgers and left the shop as he nibbled on an apple.

A Country Called the World

At home, after eating the hamburger, he lay next to the fireplace, stared at the last remaining pieces of charcoal, and slept while thinking how miserable his life was. He said to himself this sentence with a chitchat voice and went to sleep, "When your stomach is not full you cannot think; and when you get sated, you fall asleep."

A Country Called the World

A Country Called the World

Germany

The Village is not Good for Her

Based on the advice of her closest friend, she went to her aunt's house in the village to spend a few days there and relax and feel better. She also felt that, despite her ruined relationship, her long work hours and anxiety had also influenced her depression and she hoped that the rural atmosphere cheers her up and revive hope in life in her again. The day after the evening that she arrived at the village, she held *The Bread of Those Early Years*[1] in hand and began to read it while she walked in the fairly large yard of his aunt's house. It was late spring. Amy, as she placed under the shadow of a wild berry tree, suddenly felt she was at great risk. She dared not to look up. She instantly went away from the tree and sat down at the henhouse. From there, she looked at the tree and felt sad by the fact that the shadow seemed horrible to her, and then, when she looked at the chicken wire that marked the location of the hens and the roosters which had fenced one a fifth of the yard and saw that the hens and roosters inside the fence should also be kept in the iron cage that was made for them, her heart sank even more. She asked for the cause. The aunt replied with a smile that the hens and roosters were placed in the iron cage only at night when they were supposed to sleep which was good for their own health because large rats hang around there at midnight.

Amy calmed down a bit and after the aunt went out of the house, looked at the wild berry tree again. Her attention was attracted

---

[1] A book by Heinrich Böll.   [3]

to a fairly large and thick branch. He thought that if someone, say the aunty, hang herself from that branch, would the neighbor on the other side – that Amy was sure was eyeing her – come to save her? Or he would not when he saw that instead of a beautiful and tempting girl, a middle-aged and ugly woman was hanging herself, and pretended that he did not see her and went away from the window? She did not know why she should be thinking about her aunt like that. The aunt was one of the most satisfied and happiest people on earth, and Amy guessed she went out of the house to shop for the night and in honor of meeting her nephew after a few months, throw a small party with her friends. Indeed, she uses to celebrate for the smallest things, even for the first swallow that built a nest on the ceiling of her house after the end of the cold season. The *Feast of the Nests* was one of the tens of celebrations that she held every year, in addition to the parties that she arranged every week. Amy suddenly noticed the hens and the roosters were looking at her. She looked back to make sure there was no one besides her in the yard. She felt as though she was thinking loudly and the hens and the roosters had read her dirty thoughts about hanging and thus, looked at her with amazement. She was scared of herself a bit. But later, she found out that it was natural for the hens and the roosters to look as such as if they were always alert and surprised. She laughed and thought that it was better to put the book away – which she had been stuck in the first paragraph of its first page for two weeks – and take a handful of grains and pour it for the hens and the roosters, but she did not know where the grains were. She thought a little more and realized that she knew where the grains were, but she did not like to go there. The grains were in a blue bucket and the bucket was at a place like a covered backyard among other buckets at the top of which there was a wooden board. Amy got up as she was still looking at the hens and the roosters. They were not hungry and it was not necessary for Amy to go to the backyard and remember that once in her childhood, after a blunder that ended in breaking the window pane of the opposite neighbor's house, she hid at a small space between the buckets to avoid being beaten by her father. The aunt, mother and other relatives who were there on that day stopped the father, but the sound of his shouting and the footsteps on the surface of the dirt made Amy wet her pants. Why was her father like that? Because he was a military man and according to the discipline ruling over his house, none of the kids were entitled to make a blunder. It would discredit him if his children were not calm and kept a straight posture with clothes that seemingly would never get dirty. That was why Amy and her older brother and sister despised all military personnel. But Amy had gone to the village to change her mood, not to remember the bitter memories of the past. Therefore, she quietly and merrily went to the backyard, pushed the board away, and picked up a handful of grains. Space, where Amy had hidden, was still vacant. Amy wondered why, despite the abundance of old and useless dishes and gadgets piled up in the aunt's house, her aunt did not put anything there. She stepped back a little and looked at the almost hidden hallway that was as wide as a ladder. It was the same corridor that she had passed through after a stone-throwing contest between her and her cousin and the neighboring boy on the other side. She remembered the face of the neighbor's son well, who was flabbergasted and looked at the blunder she had made. Amy's childhood playmate had a stroke and died two years ago, and now, his old father was boldly eyeing Amy. Amy remembered the old man and laughed, "If you did not complain to my dad like a goat today, then I would have beaten the hell out of you!"

Then, while she laughed by the idea that had popped up in her head, she walked sideways through the narrow corridor and walked to the other side of the wild berry tree. From that angle, she could look at the old man's house without being seen. She stuck to the wall to be on the safe side, bent her head slightly, and looked at the old man's house thro the foliage. She hoped to see the old man and entertain herself a little bit by harassing him before her aunt returned. But probably the old man was not home. So, Amy went to the henhouse and poured the grains over the chicken wire for the hens and the roosters. She thought about why the hens and the roosters always attacked the grains as if they had not eaten for a long time. Then she turned her head and looked at a dog that was tied near the stairs. As far as Amy remembered, it never bothered to bark in the same position, rested its head on the ground and slept. Sometimes, it opened its eyes and looked at the newcomers, and in that situation, it looked like an alligator with only its eyes visible out of the water. But when it saw its owner, it stood up on two legs, stuck its tongue out and moved its tail. Amy looked at the dog's empty bowl. She decided to go to the kitchen and bring something for the dog too. She was hungry, even though she had breakfast half an hour ago. Because her mind was distracted as she ate breakfast and she did not have any idea about what she was eating. She went to the fridge and, in order to keep her focus and feel what she was eating, she said aloud what she was doing, "I open the refrigerator's door, well, what do we have here? Aha, honey and butter, great! I take the honey and butter, close the refrigerator's door, goddamn Michael, I spread the butter on the bread, and the honey on the butter, yum! I chew, um, um, um, the morsel went down my throat, and it reached my stomach, another one. . . Then she prepared a big morsel for the dog. When the dog saw her, got up and ate it from her hand. Amy cuddled it and it fell flat on the ground again. The hens and the roosters had eaten the grains, but as Amy thought, they seemed as if they never got sated and had gathered in front of the chicken wire and looked at Amy as if they were waiting for a miracle on her part. Amy wanted to take the rooster out of the fence, put it on her legs and stroke it. The rooster saw Amy's hand and went to her. Amy pulled it out of the fence and stroked its neck and back, and was really delighted by its crowing while her hand was on its back. She returned the rooster to the fenced area and picked her book up again. She began to read loudly as if she was reading the book for the animals in the yard. After reading every sentence, she looked at the dog and then at the hens and the roosters, and again at the dog. A little later, she heard the sound of closing the door of the opposite house. She got up and while pretending that she did not know the old man was looking at her, shook her ass and went inside the house. She opened the window a little to see whether the old man was still there. The old man was staring at the yard. Amy could clearly imagine the old man had pressed his loins firmly to the wall and waited to see her. She got out of the house, and as she pretended not to have seen the old man, s climbed the wild berry tree. She crawled to a branch that was closer to the old man's line of sight and began to eat the berries seductively. She picked the berry, looked at it with an open mouth, then put it on her tongue. A bit later, her lips were red and black. In order to remove the stickiness from her hands, she licked her fingers to the end. He skirt was pushed to the side and one side of her left leg, which was in full view of the old man, was completely exposed up to her panties. She crawled a little farther to pick a cluster of large berries and a small branch scratched her leg. Instead of a long and loud *Auch!*, she emitted a few short and successive moans. Amy was seducing the man and felt happy by taking revenge due to the fact that the old man was watching and suffering. Suddenly, the branch made a sound. She had gone too far and before she had a chance to return, she realized that she had screamed and fell on the ground. She did not want to see the old man in that situation at all. Nothing serious happened. Only her hands were hurting a bit. She cried as she had fallen on her side on the ground. She slowly got up, shook herself clean, washed her face and hands, picked her book and went inside. Out of the window, she saw in complete disbelief that the old man was laughing and a little later, his laughter grew louder and louder. Amy laughed too and raised the sound of her laughter so that the old man did not think that she did not know he had been eyeing her. She wanted to make the old man feel embarrassed and ashamed. The aunt returned home. Amy fashioned up and went to meet her with a smile to take the shopping bag from her hand. The old man had returned to the window and looked at the yard. Amy looked at him angrily but when the aunt saw the old man, she pitied him and sympathetically called him *the poor guy* in the kitchen; and before Amy wondered why she was pitying him, she said that the old man was blinded because of the blood sugar, and since he had lost his child he had lost his mind as well and sometimes laughed and sometimes cried loudly.

She said that he had that habit of standing by the window. It was too much for Amy and she suddenly felt she was more upset and more disappointed than before. She wanted to return home as soon as possible. As she realized she could never get even with the old man and take revenge of the past, she felt she was the world's worst loser. She could only manage to control herself and told the aunt that she was going to remove something that had stuck in her eye. She went to another room and cried, away from her aunt's prying eyes. As she calmed down, she preferred to think that she was supposed to spend a few days happily in the aunt's house, and as her friend put it, do not care about anything at all. She went to the aunt's side and began washing the turkey and vegetables. The aunt kissed her and went out again. Amy did not know where she was going. She just heard that she would return soon. The moment she went out, Amy instantly shut the water tap and went into the yard and looked at the old man. Then, when she was convinced that the old man was really blind and crazy, she returned inside. The time passed quickly and Amy knew that her five-day leave would end soon and she had to go back to the town. With the pain in her elbow, it was difficult not to ask herself why she had come to the village from the start. She was afraid of the place. She thought that she could not ignore everything and do not think about a solution to her problems, the psychological trauma caused by ruining her relationship with Michael, too much work, and her anxiety and fear of an unknown future, and it would be better to find a solution. She wanted to return to her home in Düsseldorf, and think about her problems right there. The village had occupied her mind in a strange way and showed her things that were not good and messed up with her thoughts. She thought how stupid she was to think a change of location could be a solution for her bad mood. The problem that had occupied her mind at the town could not be solved at the village. At least, that was true for her. So, she immediately got up, packed up, and before the aunt returned, wrote on a piece of paper that an emergency had arisen and she had to go back. She put the paper on the table and got out of the house.

A Country Called the World

Spain

The Last Race

Rosalia and Miguel thought they were having a little chat, but the abrupt Rosalia's laughter caused by excitement made every passerby who walked in front of the horses' stable to sharpen his ears, and with a little care, one could hear what was being exchanged between them – which mostly consisted of kisses and cuddles than words.

Russalia held Miguel's face between her two hands and said, "Maybe if you did not cross your hands on your chest and put them on your face, it would not have happened."

Miguel exaggerated a smile to make his broken tooth more visible. Then, as he had thrown his hand around Rosalia's waist, said, "I need my hands more than my teeth!"

There was a horse race on the next day evening, and Miguel, who for a few months had been known to run for the first prize at all costs, always got the second place with a very short distance from a horse rider from Castelldefels. When he realized that the next day's race was the last race with the presence of the Castelldefels horse rider and thereafter he would leave Spain forever, he promised to himself and Rosalia to do his best to be the first in that race.

Miguel went to his Appaloosa horse and stroked its face and said, "I will definitely win the race tomorrow! Is it not so, my boy?"

A Country Called the World

Rosalia, who stood on the other side of the white marble-like horse and stroked its long mane, said, "Our horse has become old. It is short of breath."

Miguel picked up the bucket to pour water in it. When he returned to the horse with the bucket full of water, he said, "My horse has a lot of experience and will eventually help me win. I am glad that when my horse runs at a very short distance from the first horse, the third horse and other people's horses are at a far distance from us."

While looking at the horse's saddle, his mind was busy by the thought that perhaps his horse and his rival's horse determined the distance between each other in advance, because whenever the rival as the first winner passed the finish line, Miguel was at the second place by just the length of the head of a horse behind him.

Rosalie was looking for something near the fodder as she whispered a rural song. She said as she searched, "Did not you see the apple basket?"

Miguel did not answer. He stroked the horse's neck and his mind was still busy.

At the corner of their small stable, Rosalia pulled the apple basket from under the fodder and after picking up and eating an apple with her meaty hand, aimed its leftover at Miguel. It did not hit Miguel but threw him out of his thoughts. Miguel looked at Rosalia with laughter and said, "Do not eat it alone!" and held up his hands to grab the apple that Rosalia would throw at him.

Rosalia picked up the apple and said, "First, tell me what were you thinking?!"

A Country Called the World

Miguel: "Incidentally, right now I was thinking that before you threw the apple's leftover at me, what I was thinking about!"

Rosalia crossed her eyes in confusion, which she always did and her face looked funny.

Rosalia: "I see two of you! For which one should I throw the apple?"

Miguel: "I need the apple for the horse. Toss it!"

Rosalia: "Which horse? This one or that one?!"

Finally, Miguel dumped a bucket of water on Rosalia and snatched the apple from her hand.

A quarter of an hour later,

Miguel took the horse out of the stable and mounted it. He took Rosalia's hand so she could climb too. As they were going to leave the village to go to the training area, Miguel said aloud, "This race is mine!"

His stubborn rival, who had sat at the bar, heard him and smiled. However, he recognized Miguel mostly by the neigh of his old horse and that was why he could not help laughing.

As the darkness was about to fall, Miguel and Rosalia took the horse to the stable and when they went to their house which was a little farther from the stable, Miguel said for the umpteenth time on that day, "I feel with all my heart that I will win tomorrow."

Rosalia rested her head on his lean shoulder and said, "I believe in you," and before she had a chance to say coyly, 'Aren't you cold?', so that Miguel reply with laughter, "My coat is not your size!" she realized they have arrived at the home and must prepare the dinner.

A Country Called the World

The next day afternoon, when the participants were in their places and got ready, although Miguel had not slept for three nights but did not feel tired or dizzy and it was only stress that made his body shudder, before the starting pistol went off, he glanced at the rival in whose face there was no sign of anxiety and unlike the other participants who had bent on their horses, he was casually sitting on his horse, as if he was having fun.

"Participants get in their places! Ready!" The sound of gunfire and the speeding horse that ran wildly.

After a short while that Miguel put the others behind, he realized that he was alone and there was no sign of the Castelldefels horse rider. He was upset because he did not like a victory without fierce competition.

The spectators who had bet on the Castelldefels ho rider and their number was not too few, looked at him with anger and surprise, who was moving at the very slow pace behind all others. But suddenly, he took over all of the participants at high speed, and as the shouting and cheering of the spectators grew louder, he reached Miguel. Miguel had bent over the horse so low that his chin was touching the horse's neck. He glanced at the rival's horse. The horse's eyes were full of pride like that of its owner.

Miguel not only got the second place at that race but with astonishment realized that unlike the past which he had become second at a short distance from the rival, this time he was behind him at a length equal to ten horses.

After the end of the race, Miguel insisted to Rosalia to leave him alone and took the horse to the stable and madly attacked the fodder stack and threw them to the floor. He did not calm down and pounded on the wooden pillar in the middle of the table with his fists and shouted and fell to the floor.

Near the finish line, Rosalia shaded her eyes with her hand and saw the listless face of the Castelldefels ho rider who, after passing the finish line, went far and away from the competition arena.

Shortly thereafter, Rosalia went to the stable. She saw Miguel on the floor coiled up like a snake and with fear and chills looked at the huge hole in the ceiling which was caused by the storm last week and was exactly above Miguel's head.

– "No! Miguel!"

Miguel put his injured hand on Rosalia's shoulder but could not keep his balance since he had severe pain. He slipped away but Rosalia grabbed his hand and saw he was badly injured.

She cried with a pale face, "What have you done to yourself?"

"Nothing. You were right. I should have been hurt in my hands instead of my tooth that did no good and will not do any good," said Miguel calmly, and as he shed tears like children, he crawled up on the floor again and crumbled.

A Country Called the World

A Country Called the World

Netherlands

Normal Like All Humans

Alma and Neil were two twin daughters of Mr. and Mrs. Moldik. They were perfectly identical twins such that even the corner of their right eyebrows was exactly raised to the same amount. They could never talk to each other, because whenever Alma slept, Neil woke up and whenever Neil slept, Alma woke up. The parents did their best to keep them awake at the same time but they were unsuccessful and, as the heat could not be separated from the sun, that was an impossible task. For example, a few times when Alma was asleep, Neil shook her to wake her up, but when Alma's eyelids started to move as she woke up, Neil felt sleepy and could not keep her eyes open, and when Alma woke up at the time she should have been asleep, she slept again a second later. Neil was just the same. In general, if they did not severely shake each of them in their sleep, they could not easily wake up even if they had a nightmare. Even once Mr. Moldik took both of them to the South Pole, which was on its sixth-month daytime period, so perhaps they might be awake at the same time where the day and night did not have their true meaning, but to no avail. The problem was not a matter of day or night. Anywhere on the planet, Earth Alma was awake, Neil was surely sleeping. More interestingly, when they were awake at their customarily time periods, no sleeping pill had any impact on them. There was no solution to that problem and they had to go on living like that. However, it was only Alma's life that was unusual, which she herself was unaware of it for a long time. But there were many who, like Neil, slept early in the night. The two were less likely to see their parents at the same time. So, their parents took turns to stay awake to keep their company equally and do not neglect Alma's needs over the other sister. The mother stayed awake for a week and the father stayed awake for the next week as well. Moreover, the parents had to hire a homeschooling teacher for Alma and pay him twice as much because no one was available to teach at night.

After Alma grew up, in the middle of the high school period, she decided to drop out. While the governor, the mayor, and the higher officials were aware of her problem, and even had arranged for her to go to the college, she was not interested in university education unlike her sister, and at the same time that she gave up studying she told her parents that if she was free to make a decision, she would only learn how to read and write. She showed talent in writing fiction like Neil, and then both of them co-authored great stories and became famous. Sometimes Alma wrote a story halfway through, and then Neil completed the story, and sometimes the other way round.

Since there were twelve hours for Alma and twelve hours for Neil, both had seen a part of the day and the night, but none of them wanted to switch their situation even if there was a way to do that. For Alma, the night was so calm, and the idea that perhaps one day she could walk among the crowd in daylight disturbed her. Also, it was hard for Neil to live at night and she unwittingly fell asleep right at nine o'clock.

Earlier, when they had not yet gone to the school, if they had something to say to each other, their mother would convey their words to each other. For example, Neil said, 'Mom, tell her I am not scared of the mice. How about you? Did you see my doll? You are very pretty', and Alma answered, 'I am not scared of the mice. I saw your doll; did you see my doll? You are very pretty too. I love you so much.'

Later they learned to write letters and eventually bought a small tape recorder and Alma spoke on one side of the tape and Neil spoke on the other side. It was the new normal for the people that Alma and Neil could not talk to each other in their wakefulness and that the sisters did not care as well. But when Alma started to have an affair with a boy called Tom, she wanted to live like others and that was just because Tom was tired of his odd girlfriend a bit later and was going to dump her. But Alma loved Tom so much and asked him to grant her an opportunity to find a way and experience day and night like other people.

========

Neil: "Oh, darling, do not worry. Do not take him seriously, his exhaustion justifies that. Tom's job is really hard. What's more, boys are all the same. If they feel you are digging them, they play hard to get. He will be back on his own accord. By the way, today a publisher paid for five stories in advance so we do not sell them to another one. This money is yours and I put it beside the cassette tape. Next time, lock the door of the mailbox properly. It opened before inserting the key."

Alma: "Thank you for the money. I am not feeling well. I feel I will perish if Tom leaves me. I wish I had never been friends with him. Did the herpes blister on your lip heal?"

Neil: "My dear, I wish I could be on your side so you do not feel lonely. I wish there was a way to see each other in wakefulness. The blister on my lip was healed, yes. Dad and mom complain and say it is a week you have not gone to meet them. Mom is here. Come on, tell your daughter yourself."

Mother: "Hi, sweetie. Come here as soon as possible. You are only two blocks away from us, but it seems you are living in another state! We are waiting for you. Did you hear that? Come pay a visit. I eagerly look forward to knowing how you are going to continue the previous story. A girl who can both fly and dive deep in the water, where would she live if she could choose one? If I was in her shoes, I would love to sometimes live among the birds and sometimes with the fish, but if I had to choose one, I would choose the birds. What was I going to say. . . oh! I am going to my friend rose's party tomorrow. She has just arrived at Rotterdam. The girl is awesome. She throws her party at noon so I can go too. She said she sometimes throws parties at noon just for my sake. Can I borrow your skirt? The one that you recently bought at an auction?"

Alma: "I met my parents tonight. Of course, you can wear my skirt. Just the zipper on the back is a bit hard to close and you must get the hold of it. Do not be tempted to take it out at the party! Because if you cannot pull up the zipper again, you must keep it up with your hand on your back till you reach home so that it does not fall from your body. Oh, about the story, I think the girl should live with the fish. The birds are stereotypes. She lives with the fish, and one day a fisher boy catches one of her friends. She and the other fish get upset about it, but since the fish have a poor memory, they get caught one after the other. In the end, the girl is left alone in the river and decides to fly to the sky and live among the birds, but she cannot because she had become like the fish and has grown fins and gills. That is, right when nobody else is around her and all of the fish are caught; she realizes that she herself has become a fish just when there are no longer any fish so the girl protects them from being cheated. She looks like a fish, but her memory is still as human beings. So, she never gets caught. But because she is fed up with being lonely, she decides to get herself caught. I hope you will enjoy the party."

Neil: "I'm sorry to hear that the zipper on your skirt was damaged. Do not be pessimistic. When the party was over and I came to your house to remove the skirt, the zipper could not be opened. I pulled down the zipper hard, and it snapped out. I took it to a tailor shop. I will bring it to you tomorrow. It seems that we have some disagreement for the first time! How well you finished the story! Your voice was choked and sad. I really want to see you. I worry about you. Do you want me to tell mom to come to see you?"

Alma: "No, I am fine. I also really want to see you with all my heart. I have an idea that may help us to see each other! You come to my home tomorrow at bedtime. When you sleep, I fill the tub full of water and put my head in it. I also tell Tom to come and keep my head under the water and do not let me come up, and when I am nearly dead and Tom realizes that you do not wake up, he must immediately pull my head out of the water. It is a bit risky. But it is worth trying. I feel that right at the moment that I will go unconscious, you will wake up and we will see each other and from then on, we will live an ordinary life like other people! We go around together and shop and travel. I am very excited! I do not know what to say if I see you! Darling."

Neil: "I do not know what to say. . . I am very excited too, but admit it is a very dangerous task. Let me put my head in the tub

instead of you. I do not want to see you get hurt. Let's fix it up
with Tom. I will be at your home tomorrow at eleven."

The next day, Tom and Neil went to Alma's house. Alma had
already filled the tub full of water and fell asleep in front of the
bathroom. Neil said to Tom that he should not freak out when
he saw her flailing her arms and legs and do not pull her head
out of the water. Tom had her sign a letter of consent and
repeatedly reminded her that if something happened, Neil
would bear the consequences. Then, he kept her head under the
water while trembling with fear, and looked at Alma to see
whether she woke up or not so that if there was no sign of her
awakening at all, he could immediately pull Neil's head out of
the water. A few seconds passed. Tom saw Neil had clenched
her fists, and a bit later, her fists began to open and close
repeatedly. Alma stirred. As if she was somewhere between
sleep and wakefulness. Suddenly, she woke up while grasping
her throat and Neil's shudders subsided. Tom immediately
brought up Neil's head out of the water. There was a little blood
in the water. Tom pressed the Nile's ribcage a few times and
Alma, who pretended to be mixed up, pointed out the muted
Neil's pulse and did not allow Tom to give mouth-to-mouth
respiration to her sister.

After the parents heard the news of Neil's death, Alma said that
both of them thought they could live a normal life like other
human beings and both she and her sister were very upset about
being born that way. The parents did not suspect that Alma had
poisoned the water. She had a plan to put her head in the water
the first time, and after getting no results, poison the water
afterward and ask Neil to do the same thing.

A Country Called the World

Alma returned home after nine o'clock. She thought to herself, "I am not a wicked person. I did not even know her at all. How could I feel sisterhood toward a person who I had never seen before? She was the one who had ruined my life. However, one should have died so the other could live a normal life. She had to die. Because she had experienced a normal life, and it was me who was alone, odd and tormented. Who said I hate the day? I like both day and night. I fell in love! In order to be able to live with someone, I must be like others. No. I do not regret it. I am not alone anymore. I have Tom! I saw the daytime! I saw a crowded street! I saw the people during the day! The weather was great. I want to live like the rest of the people."

A few hours passed and Alma was still deep in her thoughts to calm down her conscience. When the sun rose, Alma realized that twenty hours had passed since the time she had gone to sleep yesterday, but she has not slept yet. That day was Neil's funeral, but it did not matter to her. She looked at the clock again which showed it was 6:00 AM. She did not feel sleepy at all. She preferred to go to her parents' home. Several hours passed and they buried Neil. Alma was still awake. She thought her insomnia was rooted in fear and anxiety. But after a couple of days went by and she was still awake, she realized that the sleep had completely forsaken her and she had to be awake round the clock for eternity.

A Country Called the World

A Country Called the World

Peru

The Joy of Being the First

Alex was looking at Sheila and Sheila was looking at the ceiling.

– "You are nineteen. I can hardly believe that I am the first boy you have fallen in love with. I am not really convinced, my dear."

He whispered these words in her ear. After Alex kissed the corner of Sheila's eyes, she lifted her head from his arm and looked around. A brief glance indicating that she was looking for something that she knew where it was, but she did not have enough concentration to find it.

– "I found it."

Without looking at the floor, she picked up the cigarette pack which was next to the bedpost and sat down on the edge of the bed. She lit her cigarette using the matchbox that Alex had brought from the kitchen to the bedroom to light the candle and said, "It is a secret why I did not have a lover up to this time and you are my first lover."

Alex asked with discomfort, "What is the reason that you do not trust me yet, after great lovemaking?"

Sheila looked at him sympathetically and while stroking his hand, she said, "No, my dearest. I do not distrust you. Of course, I will tell you why."

A Country Called the World

Before she disclosed her secret, she got up and pulled the room's curtain away. The pale winter sunlight lit up Alex's tiny house. Alex's house was small but had large windows. If one stood next to the window, his torso from almost the knee up would be visible from the outside. Sheila stood in front of the window for a while and thought deeply. A disabled young man on a wheelchair, who had to ride on the side of the street due to a damaged section on the sidewalk, looked at the window. He stared for a few moments at Sheila's body and went away with a smile. The young man's smile meant that 'How lucky are those two pieces of clothes that are stuck to your body."

Sheila sat down again on the edge of the bed. She was looking for something again.

Alex said, "Use that piece of paper as an ashtray."

She pulled the piece of paper closer to her and poured the ash on it.

Someone pounded on the door, "... Mr. Bonster! I have come to clean the house. Please open the door if you are awake. Oh... I will be back in an hour. Also, make ready for the past two months' rent in an hour. Madam is very angry."

Alex put his hand on his lips as a sign of keeping silent. Madonna, the forty-three-year-old servant of the old-fashioned three-story apartment where Alex lived was always kind. At all times, she talked calmly and kindly even in anger. Alex had to pay the outstanding rent to that nagging old woman who was his landlord. A wicked woman, who would deliberately cut off the house's power in the evening if Alex did not pay the rent on time. Some of the things that annoyed Alex was that the apartment was no big deal and was built at the Piura's suburbs.

A Country Called the World

- "Now, tell me your secret."

Sheila put off her cigarette and lest she might be heard, spoke with a hushed voice, "My stepfather was badly addicted to alcohol. He was a foul-smelling fat couch potato who took baths once a month. He beat my mom every day and forced her to prostitution. After my mother committed suicide, the creditors, that is, the gambling partners of Joe, threw him in jail. I was six at that time. Thereafter, the newlywed Joe's younger brother took custody of me. Rio was no different than his reckless brother, but he did not bet on his wife and did not sell her. But when I turned fourteen. . ."

She went to the window again and this time, put her hands on her waist like pregnant women. A teardrop rolled on her pretty cheek and fell on the floor.

– "One night when I was sleeping in my room, three drunken men came for me. I noticed someone was caressing my hair. I tried to cry out but a hand wrapped tightly in front of my mouth. I was scared and passed out. But I was lucky and stayed intact. When I came to my senses, I realized that a neighbor who had long been monitoring Rio's suspicious behavior had called the cops. Rio started shooting at the police but got killed. I volunteered to go to the eldercare facility to work there and at least secure a meal and a roof above me. I worked at the eldercare for four years for free, then I moved here from Columbia with the support of a physician. He was kind and sympathetic, and when I told him my story and said that I wanted to leave that place, he gave me some money that I could spend for a month. I came here to start anew. I never liked boys and men. I am afraid of all of them. I have been living in the opposite building for about a year. During this one year, I made a living by nursing a single old lady who is my landlord. When I saw you. . . an innocent face and feeble body! As if I had left my childhood and adolescence behind in your face. You were oozing kindness and innocence. When you waved for me last week from your room, well, I really do not know why I fell in love with you. I do not know why I think you are different than all of them. . ." she choked with emotion and could not help crying anymore.

Alex grabbed her hand and that was enough for Sheila to jump hard into his lap.

– "Get up and tidy up yourself, it is time to go."

Sheila looked at her face in the mirror and gathered up her hair. But Alex was still sitting on the bed watching her. He was very happy. It did not matter to him what had happened to Sheila and the only thing that mattered was . . . what a tempting scene! One of those scenes that could make all men drool. A brunette with long, brown hair and black eyes. Though those colors were known to everyone, they seemed mysterious and unknown in the context of Sheila's hair and pupils of her eyes. She looked so beautiful that by seeing her, one could regret being created as such. A body was so curved and sculptured that it seemed it was only created to melt the men's stamina! How could one ignore that? That Alex was the first person to embrace all that beauty. He was the first lover of that beauty goddess. He was the first one and for Alex, that was sweeter and better than anything.

He thought, 'What a good feeling is it to be the first!' and he was very happy.

Sheila was ready. Alex got out of the bed cheerfully and promptly put on his clothes that hung on the back side of the door. Then he opened the room's door for Sheila and said: "I am so happy I met you. See you later."

Sheila stood in front of him up and wondered, "Do not you come out?!"

Alex replied, "No, not with you. I will go alone. Please go before my landlord shows up because I have to go too."

Sheila said, "Oh, I do not understand you, Alex!"

Alex scratched his face and thought a bit to find a way to tell her what he had in mind.

He said, "I just wanted to know what it is like to be the first one. You know. I do not know how to put it. Since childhood, I have always been one of the last ones. I never got the first rank in the school and college courses or in any competitions I participated in. I wanted to know how it feels to be the first. What does a person feel when he gets the first place in the school and college or gets the championship ranking in a competition? An exemplary student, exemplary employee, exemplary child. . . what really a person feels when he is acknowledged for being the first?! Even in relationships, there have always been people before me. I do not know. Perhaps the girls who were with me had experienced love too early and at a very young age, or maybe I came of age too late. But now I am very happy. Finally, I experienced being the first! I am the first love of someone!"

Sheila stared at him with astonishment, picked up her purse and got out of the house, but at the doorway, she turned back and spit on Alex's face and rushed down the stairs. After Sheila went away, Alex wiped his face and rejoiced since he had experienced being the first.

A Country Called the World

A Country Called the World

Turkey

Thirsty to Create Memories

Parihan, "Last night, you told it up to your admittance in the university."

"When I was admitted at university, I moved to Istanbul with my parents," said Dr. Dwigo Uxel, as he slowly raised her bed, "For village people like my parents, Istanbul means confusion and stress and for country women like me, Istanbul is a launching pad for progress. Since I was admitted in a very good university to study medicine, seemingly my parents were not too upset by being far from me, but I knew that they pretended so to make it more comfortable for me to tolerate their being away. Of course, I felt sad. After they saw me off to the university, they returned to Cihane. The last thing my father said before going back was, 'Take care of yourself'. Until that moment, I did not know how a simple phrase could have so many different meanings. In that context, 'Take care' meant come see us as much as you can since we cannot live without you and that was the truth. Just the day after I went to college, my mother fell ill.

When I saw my mother in that situation, I decided to drop out of college and the next time, choose the nearest college to the home. But they did not allow me and I was not so determined. My mother's disease was a psychiatric condition. Depression.

I had to talk to her with a serious and firm tone and reassure her that if she got restless again, I definitely would not go to the college again. I got on the bus and when I was on my way back to Istanbul, again the last word I heard from my father was, 'Take care of yourself'. . . well, if you feel tired, I will tell the rest later."

Parihan, "No, no. As you see, I am all ears and I want you to go on."

Dr. Uxel, "Two weeks after I went to college, I spent almost all of my money. We were four people in the dormitory who are now working together in this hospital. The university food was not good. Each of us contributed and participated in buying foodstuff. When I was penniless, I went to the library in the morning before my friends woke up and pretended that I was busy learning French and would have breakfast later. I did the same at lunchtime and dinnertime. Sometimes I said I had eaten out and went on hungry and sometimes I snitched my roommates' food when they were not around. Being poor is worse than loneliness. It is poverty that begets loneliness, methinks. Someone who lives far from his family for the sake of the university must count every penny meticulously. She must even control her falling ill. One should not get sick when there is no money. She ought to get sick when there is enough money to spend on the treatment. Then she may allow herself to catch a cold, suffer from food poisoning, and feel like it is time to operate on her appendicitis or any other disease. At that point, I realized the meaning of 'Take care of yourself' that my father said in the bus terminal, which meant be careful not to get sick when you do not have the money, let alone going out or buying something. Because in that case, you have to borrow and double up your misery. And I am certain that a person cannot be happy in two circumstances. One: when. . ."

A Country Called the World

Parihan interrupted him and said, "When she is not healthy, and two?"

Dr. Uxel, "Two: when she is in debt. A debt that could hardly be paid back."

Parihan: "You mean it has the same impact on one's happiness as health?"

Dr. Uxel, "Of course not. Indebtedness makes you worry most of the time, which in this case you certainly cannot enjoy life as you should. The first few days that I was impoverished, whenever I talked to my parents on the phone and they asked whether I had money, I answered I was fine as far as I could. Because my dad was a second-hand dealer and his financial situation was not so good.

"I could not keep it to myself and after two weeks of pennilessness, when they contacted me and asked whether I was in need of something, I said that I needed a little money. I said it in a way that they do not worry and do not think to themselves perhaps they had paid me less than the amount of money I actually needed. But my dad got the point and thereafter, he was going to send me more money. Three days after sending me the money, he asked me on the phone whether I had received my money or not. At the end of the conversation, when he was going to hang up, he said: 'Study well! We miss you so much . . . hope to see you soon! Take care!' I immediately understood the meaning of this 'take care'. That is, 'My dear daughter, you know that I am a second-hand dealer and I thought the amount I gave you at first was enough for a month. But I see that it was not enough. This time I sent you more and to do that, I had to raise the price of my merchandise. I sold the gas oven, furniture and chairs are a bit more expensive. But do not worry at all! I am a second-hand dealer and nobody can protest. Even if I sell my goods more expensive, everyone still thinks the price is reasonable! But this is not good in terms of conscience. So, be careful that you will not expect me to do that the next time. . .' and actually, it happened just once. Till the next time, I started working at the university library and could make the ends meet. I realized that I will worry no more when I hear those 'Take cares' from my dad.

"I met Mustafa two months after entering the college. He frequently came to the library and met me. One day, at the end of working hours, I left college and walked to the dormitory and he called me. When I returned and looked at him, he said, 'I just wanted to say take care of yourself'. Then he waived and went away. How different was the meaning of this statement! I was not waiting for a bad incident anymore, and as I figured out later, his 'take care of yourself', meant 'I love you and it matters to me that nothing bad happens to you', and I was careful not to have a stroke because of my love for him!

"We got married and still after twenty-five years, when he tells me, 'take care of yourself', I feel my heart grows so large that if it could be divided among all those who need a heart transplant, it will easily satisfy it.

"Well, my memories are finished. During these fourteen nights, I tried to tell you my most important memories."

"You mean no other memories are left?!" asked Parihan.

Dr. Uxel: "Usually, good and unforgettable memories rarely happen. I must go now. I will be back in a week."

Parihan: "How late. . ."

Dr. Uxel: "The week will pass in the blink of an eye."

Parihan: "Yes, for you. But for me time is an endless tunnel, every minute takes as long as a year. Can you get back sooner?"

Dr. Uxel: "I will try to get back sooner."

Parihan: "What you mean by sooner?"

"It is in the next six days and twenty-three hours and fifty-nine minutes!" replied Dr. Uxel laughingly.

Parihan turned her face away from the doctor. The doctor stroked and kissed Parihan's face.

After a few seconds, Parihan said, "You have to fetch me something on your way back."

Dr. Uxel: "I will bring you anything you want."

Parihan: "Memory! Bring me the memories. The memories of the week that you are not here. Bitter or sweet makes no difference."

Dr. Uxel: "I have no control over the memories. If something happens that could be a memory, I will surely do it," she kissed her face and head again and added, "Be a good girl. I will be back very soon."

"I will be waiting for you right here! Take care of yourself!" said Parihan sarcastically.

A Country Called the World

A Country Called the World

Canada

Fear of Darkness

The power was cut off, all the eight-year-old children screamed. Brad and Bernard were going to run to their parents but they felt they were facing a wall and they would hit it with the slightest movement. Susan and Lucy embraced each other at the spot where they were sitting and began to cry. Eugene, though he was very scared and crying quietly, could remember where his friends were standing or sitting just a few seconds before power was cut and imagine their faces in the dark how they cried. He had already seen them crying at the school many times.

All of them had cried many times because of cheating at games, mocking each other, fighting, and frightening one another with scary masks. But Eugene did not know, and until then had not seen, how his friends cried when they were horrified in the dark. He thought his own type of crying due to the fear of darkness was different than other times. The veins on his neck had swollen, his eyelids had closed with more pressure and his mouth was wide open as much as possible, but his throat emitted a muffled sound, like the faint squeak of a mouse in a trap. Brad was weeping louder than others. As if he expected the others to cry like him, and when he noticed each of his friends were shouting and crying according to their own style, he raised his crying sound incrementally, like an orchestra conductor who crazily waves his wand in the air in front of the audience because of the inconsistency of the members of the group and cannot accept that the group has screwed everything. From the living room's point of view, where the adults had gathered, one could imagine that as soon as the house was dark, lava was poured under the kids' feet and the same perception could justify their ignorance of the adults who constantly advised, 'What the hell is going on! Hush! Be quiet!'. Perhaps they were not so terrified and did not cry if, before the power outage, Brad had not blurted out a bunch of lies about seeing a jinn and how not to be afraid of it just to show off before the girls.

Within almost three minutes, Mr. Gibson, Catherine's father, lit the gas lamp with a lighter. The room brightened up and the kids and ran to their parents. Eugene was really terrified more than everyone, both because of the darkness which had helped to visualize the creatures that Brad was talking about, and because at the peak of the noise and ruckus, he felt someone kissed his cheek.

After all the kids took shelter in the safe haven of their parents' bosoms and calmed down, they still did not realize that Catherine was not afraid and did not cry at all. She was sitting calmly in her mother's lap, looking at Eugene.

Among them, first Eugene lifted his head from his mother's chest and looked around. The adults' smiling faces, the mothers who stroked their children's heads, his frightened friends who were clinging to their parents as if they wished their clothing change color like a chameleon so the feeling of terror miss them and go far away from them, playing cards and bottles, his father's smile with the usual 'You are a grown-up person now", his mother's smile with the usual 'Look at Catherine, learn a tad from her", and Catherine's poker face who was looking at him with her blue eyes. Even after his fear was completely diminished, he did not notice Catherine's horny eyes and in response to her smile, he foolishly whispered in his mother's ears that Catherine must have been possessed by a Jinni.

Two days after that incident and after the weekend, Catherine saw Eugene was alone at a corner of the schoolyard and went to him and said, "That night scared the hell out of you!"

Eugene: "I swear I sensed the jinn. I have been sleeping with my parents since that night."

Catherine: "But I was not scared at all. Neither by Brad's mumbo-jumbo nor by the darkness."

Eugene: "Perhaps you were not afraid because you were at your own home."

Catherine: "I am not afraid of the dark at all, even if I am at Brad grandma's old house. She says the Jinn hang around there every night."

Eugene: "None of Brad's words were false. One of those same jinn kissed me!"

Catherine: "But the Jinn that he was talking about were all evil and terrible. If it was one of them, it should have gouged out your eye instead of kissing you!"

Eugene looked at her worriedly.

Catherine: "Maybe they like you and come back for you again!"

Eugene could hardly keep himself from bursting into tears in broad daylight.

Catherine: "Did you tell anyone that you saw the jinn?"

A Country Called the World

Eugene: "I told my parents the same night. My mom said it was her. I know she was lying so I do not freak out. My mom lied to me, is it not so?"

Catherine: "Did not you tell anyone other than your parent?"

Before Eugene had a chance to answer, Brad and Bernard came and by pulling his cheek and casting a meaningful look at Catherine, hinted that he should not have told them about the kiss. Perhaps if the school break time did not finish, Brad and his brother stayed there and continued making fun of them. As Brad and Bernard left, Eugene said, "We have to go to the classroom."

"Come with me," said Catherine.

Eugene went to the far side of the school with Catherine. No one could see them.

"Close your eyes," demanded Catherine.

Eugene was amazed and scared, but he closed his eyes. He felt the same kiss again.

Catherine stepped away a bit and said, "Never fear the darkness," and went toward the classroom.

Eugene put his hand on his cheek and walked slowly behind her. He did not know whether he had any special interest in her before the kiss, but afterward, he eagerly wanted her. He wanted to experience the darkness with her again. He wished that suddenly everywhere turned dark so he could run to Catherine and embrace her. If he walked a bit faster, he could catch up with Catherine and hold her hands all the way to the classroom, but he did not do it. The kiss had occupied his mind so deeply that he could walk behind Catherine for quite a few days and nights without moving closer to her.

A Country Called the World

In the classroom, Eugene thought about Catherine's treatment of him in the past and realized that her behavior was more than just a casual friend and classmate. When he needed a pencil sharpener, eraser, pencil or paper, it was always Catherine who handed him what he needed, way faster than the guy sitting next to Eugene. While Catherine sat on the first chair and Eugene on the last one, she handed him the cheat sheet by any possible means. The selfish Catherine, the arrogant Catherine, who did not give a cheat sheet to anyone except Eugene. She always invited Eugene to share her food. All of that aside, undoubtedly if Catherine had not kissed him for the second time, the naive and humble boy of the Grace Park Elementary School never noticed her fondness.

This naivety, and largely the stupidity of Eugene, disappointed Catherine at first but then, made her more interested in him. Maybe Eugene was an ordinary child and too much bullying by most of his classmates had made him shine in Catherine's blue eyes like the sun. Although Brad and Bernard were more stylish and handsome, they could never attract Catherine's attention. Brad always used throwaway tattoos on his hands. Catherine had witnessed for many times that the two brothers bump into female classmates and ogle them from the back of the classroom. Even once, the two brothers made a bet that could approach the young mathematics teacher and touch her body, and Bernard won. One day, he faked stomach cramps at the classroom and as he cried and was carried to the principal's office with the help of the female teacher, maintained body contact to her boobs and belly. However, Brad once was slapped hard by the fat and meaty hand of a girl at a higher grade, but the slap just made the brothers smarter to proceed with better planning.

A Country Called the World

– "I sleep in my room tonight."

It was just seven o'clock in the evening when Eugene said that to his parents before dinner and went to his room. The curtain slipped and covered the window, the light went off, and as Eugene had stood with closed eyes next to the switch, he whispered, "I love darkness. It is not horrible at all."

While he was sure that it was Catherine who had kissed him in the dark, but he was still somewhat afraid and anxious. He was about to step away from the switch but a force pinned him down right there. A force that had authority over each one of his cells and even did not allow him to open his eyes. He tied to think of Catherine.

When the last bell rang, Eugene went toward Catherine to sit next to her on the bus. Catherine noticed that Eugene had finally got hooked, so she played hard to get and waited for Eugene to approach her. Therefore, she ignored his gesture when the last bell rang and pretended she was busy packing up her bag and books. Eugene waited a moment for the kids to leave the classroom. In order to send Bard and Bernard away, he told them they were supposed to report to Mr. Carner, their teacher. When everyone left the classroom, Eugene went to Catherine and without saying anything, lowered his head and got out of the classroom with her. Catherine was looking straight ahead and the shy Eugene, before they reach the entry and exit gate of the school building, awkwardly turned and looked back twice. He tried to match his steps with that of Catherine's such that the sound of footsteps of only one person could be heard and the *tatap tatap* noise change to a simple *tap*. It did not take long for such a thing to happen. To attenuate the noise of his own footsteps relative to that of Catherine's, he was cautious to put

A Country Called the World

his feet slowly on the ground. He was extremely thrilled and thus, had clung to his backpack's straps so firmly as if he expected something like a parachute pop out of it to save him from being shattered to pieces due to extreme excitement. In fact, he was as excited as a paratrooper who has not yet opened his parachute. He forced himself to check his surroundings from the corner of his eye. They were a few steps away from the schoolyard's gateway. They had to reach the two vacant seats behind the driver before Brad and Bernard saw them. Eugene raised his head and walked away from Catherine with big strides and looked at the children who had lined up to get on the bus. Brad and Bernard were at the end of the queue and their chit-chat showed they had an awful plan in mind. Eugene was lucky because those two were supposed to return home with their mother since they had put thumbtacks on the driver's seat and were banned from the school bus service for a week. Eugene did not know that at that moment, just two days had passed from their one-week ban, and breathed a sigh of relief as he saw Mrs. Jefferson grabbed her sons' hands, removed them from the queue and took them away.

Eugene got on the bus first to sit next to the window. Catherine had only ten minutes to show him her name and Eugene's name that she had written on the paper a while ago and Eugene would arrive at home in the next twenty minutes. Eugene leaned back and folded his arms on his chest. As the bus started out, he moved closer and closer to Catherine. Catherine had sat in the same manner and preferred to move in accordance with his pace. Eugene stuck his arm to her arm. This time, he tried to match his respiration cycle with hers. A moment later, he took Catherine's fingertips from under his armpit and hoped that Catherine put her head on his shoulder. Catherine held the full extent of Eugene's hand and as she had likewise folded her arms on her chest, said, "If you love me, you should never be afraid of darkness."

Eugene pressed her hand and said, "I promise not to fear it anymore."

Catherine forcefully separated her hand from his hand and pulled out the piece of paper from the bag. Eugene saw his own name that was glued to the name of Catherine with a heart. The page frame was decorated with several flower branches which clearly showed that Catherine had not painted them. Her older sister had painted the framed artwork and only the name and the heart were Catherine's work. Eugene took the love-immersed paper from her and promised to bring her something like that the next day. He put the paper in his bag and immediately folded his arms on his chest and showed his hand from underneath his armpit to grab Catherine's hand again. Catherine laughed and placed her hand on her knee and said, "No need to fold your arms!"

Eugene grabbed her hand and asked respectfully, "May I kiss you?"

Catherine looked at the driver. Then returned to look at her classmates. When she saw the situation was secure, she took the pencil out of her bag and threw it in front of Eugene's foot and imitated Eugene's courteous tone, "My pencil fell under your feet. Would you please give it to me?!"

As Eugene bent forward to pick up the pencil, Catherine bent down too, pushed back her hair behind her ear and moved her cheek forward. Eugene kissed her gently.

A Country Called the World

In the darkness, Eugene tried hard to clearly review Catherine's face and the bus events, but he did not succeed. He imagined Catherine on the bus, but suddenly her teeth grew bigger and her eyes popped out of their sockets. The bus driver's eyes turned white and without pupils. Instead of the song Blowing in the Wind[1] that the driver was listening to, scream sound was broadcast from the bus. His classmates laughed chillingly and devoured each other, and the bus turned into a large coffin.

The surge of this delirium scared the hell out of Eugene and forced him to cry out and call his parents. Eugene's eyes were still closed as the father opened the door and light penetrated into the room. Only one minute had passed from the time that Eugene was in the dark. In the darkness of the evening! Darkness that thanks to the street lights, brightened his room so that one could easily see the bed, the airplane hanging from the ceiling, the bookshelf, and his guitar. Eugene might not be afraid at all if he just opened his eyes.

---

[1] Blowing in the Wind, a song by Bob Dylan, the American singer, songwriter, author , and poet.

A Country Called the World

A Country Called the World

Brazil

The Secretaries

Although Fernanda went there early morning she was disappointed to realize she was still about a half an hour walking distance to the head of the queue. She did not know that many of the people had been standing there since the night before and had not bat tedan eyelid for the fear of someone taking their turn. The length of the line increased by the second. It was 11:05 and the air was getting warmer and warmer. Fernanda tilted herself to look back. She saw a large crowd behind her who was standing across the long distance between the two unfinished houses. She pitied them because she was standing at a spot where she could at least lean on the wall. During the five hours that she was standing there, the queue moved forward by just 16 people. It was not known what was going on in the office that the line was moving so slowly. She was sure that besides Sao Paulo girls, girls from other cities were there too. Well, it was great! The line moved another step forward. Perhaps her turn would be around sunset or at most, the night. Again, she wondered whether all of them had come there for the secretary job. Was there actually no other job for them except being employed as a secretary in a small coffee-distribution office? Perhaps not, because in such case, she would be among those who left the place. In fact, she wished there was another job and she could leave that place. Her feet were tired and she yawned frequently. No one talked to anyone, and everyone hated one another. Fernanda did not like anyone either. A few minutes later, a petite girl who had stood behind

A Country Called the World

Fernando quietly asked her about the college in which she had studied and what were her skills.

When she heard Fernanda's short and cheesy answer, she said, "It seems all of us have been so lonely and isolated that we have got used to isolation and cannot stand anyone. At least, let you and me be friends."

Fernanda turned back and told her, "Sometimes, one gets disgusted of life when one sees a lot of people like herself, not because one is alone and nobody understands her!"

The petite girl's heart broke and faked a smile to hide the tears that had gathered in her eyes. After a few seconds, Fernanda realized how harshly she had spoken to her and was upset by her own creepy behavior. The previous night, when she was sleeping in the homeless shelter, she did not have that opinion and she felt good about not being alone and other people were in the homeless shelter like her. Therefore, she turned and hugged the petite girl, "Sorry! I did not mean it! You know, I have been here since dawn and it has really tested my patience."

The petite girl cried on Fernanda's shoulder which was covered by cheap but clean underwear. Since nobody was talking in the queue except for them, Fernanda thought it was the law of the queue. So, to be on the safe side, she whispered in the ears of the petite girl that she would better stand in her place and do not cry again. Then, she thought to herself if the head of the office would say, for example, you have to fight each other and the last survivor would get hired here, were they willing to do that? But suddenly, the two girls behind the petite girl started arguing.

– "Hey, you bitch! Wake up! Do not put your head on my back."

A Country Called the World

When the girl behind her heard this, she slapped her hand, grabbed her hair and pulled her out of the queue. Then, she went back to the queue and because she was tired, she fell asleep again in the standing position. The beaten girl realized that she had been kicked out of the line, so she picked up a stone from the ground, and while Fernanda and the petite girl and the two girls behind the sleeping girl covered their faces with their hands, threw it fiercely and with all of her power toward the sleeping girl. Fernanda felt something like a pebble hit the back of her hand and when she looked down, she saw three of the sleeping girl's teeth were fallen on the ground and their bloodstream was running toward them. The scared petite girl was clinging to Fernanda and dared not to look back. The murderer girl returned to her spot. For several hours, that is, till 4:00 PM that the queue moved forward by ten persons, Fernanda did not look behind her. She thought that if the murdered girl did not push the killer out of the queue and treated her the same way at the same place, she would have certainly been alive and her blood did not imprint the tracks of her and the petite girl and several other girls who were standing at the back. When she dared to look back, she saw that the victim had crumpled and fallen on the ground and others were at their places in the queue, indifferent to her.

The murderer's face looked very normal and she did not seem to have committed a murder and was somewhat proud. The petite girl asked Fernanda to check the back of her shirt for blood stains. Fernando saw the blood stains and told her that she had better walk sideways when she entered the office up to sitting on the chair. They were seemingly slightly sensitive to the people's appearance which could be inferred from their mandatory dress code including wearing a white shirt, black skirt, pantyhose, and black low heel shoes. Fernanda had already said to herself that it was still good they only described their colors and dressing style and for example, did not say what brand you must wear. Indeed, they would have done so if they were supposed to fight for employment.

At 16:15, a little girl who was running slowly, counting the people in the line, reached Fernanda: one hundred and two, one hundred and three. She pointed at Fernanda and said loudly, "Tonight at twelve o'clock, we will reach here. The rest of you go and come tomorrow. "

The petite girl looked at Fernanda enviously. When Fernanda - who moments ago was thinking about whether she would get a place at the homeless shelter if she quit the line, and on the other hand, if she stayed in the queue it was unclear whether she could get the job - saw the look of the petite girl, stayed in the queue. Some people behind her left the queue but some people wanted to stay there until the next day. A moment after the little girl ran back, the girl in front of Fernanda fell backward. Fernanda stepped aside and looked at her. Her pulse had stopped. The petite girl who was going to stand there till the next day found that out. The petite girl was lucky that there was no one behind her; otherwise, if someone saw her switch her place with a dead person to stand behind Fernanda would beat the hell out of her. Why others do not take her place? She changed her bloody shirt with the dead girl's shirt which fitted her well. It was still too early to celebrate, but the petite girl could not help not to snap her fingers thanks to her luck that kept her in the queue and got her turn on the same day. When Fernanda saw the person in front of her, she realized all the people standing in the queue were not just young girls. The person in front of her had white hair and a curved posture, and Fernanda did not know what she wished for by standing there.

It was twelve midnight and right at the time when Fernanda could no longer stand on her legs, it was her turn. As she walked up to the seven or eight stair steps of the office, she tried not to fall down and get injured or break her leg, since she could not hide the broken and lame leg. She entered the office. As the old woman who was sitting there saw her, she laughed and told her that she was really lucky. Fernanda sat on the chair. The old woman filled a glass of wine for her. Fernanda said she did not drink wine and the old woman asked her why.

Fernando said, "I do not like something external penetrate into my body to make me happy artificially."

The old woman said, "You must try everything at least once to see whether you like it or not."

Fernanda thought her words seem logical. When she took a sip, she felt the wine was very bitter and distasteful.

The old woman noticed her uptight complexion and said, "The first time, always one's mouth feels a bad aftertaste," and went to the refrigerator and added, "Here, we are never short of foodstuff."

Fernanda was very delighted to know the abundance of food had caused the refrigerator to bulge since it was not clear what the last time she had eaten was. The old woman waited for Fernanda to be sated. Fernanda was optimistic and thought since the old woman had kept her there, she would surely hire her. But when she thought more, she realized that maybe the line moved so slowly because someone was eating there. Therefore, she stopped eating and asked the old woman to tell her about the job. The old woman asked her about her academic degree and when she found out that Fernanda had not gone to school at all, she told her again how lucky she really was, but this time she meant something else. The old woman told her she had to sit at the desk and interview the applicants. That is, to ask about their academic degree and then, send them out of the door behind her. That door opened to the entrance of the town and everyone who got out through it would be back in the queue, whose head's whereabouts was not clear. The old woman told Fernanda that no one should get disappointed there; their mere standing in the line meant that they were doing something, so they were respected. She added that some people stay so long in that long queue that they get old and, despite in that age they did not fit the job, they still did not lose their hope and continue their endeavor with determination. Fernanda was happy that she did not become such a vain person and said to herself if the old lady who entered the office before he was in the line again and she certainly were, her turn would be at least in the next forty years and the next forty years meant her third time. Until then, she would be a hundred and thirteen if she survived. She was also relieved of the thought that after the rejection of the petite girl for the next 40 years, she would not see her again because they had become friends and she did not like to see her again a moment later.

The old woman said she could eat and sleep for as long as she wanted a day in and day out. Fernanda realized why the queue was moving slowly and said it aloud. The old woman laughed and admitted it and said that was because she slept a lot. She said sometimes to escape boredom and just for fun, she asked the applicants to try to count the hair growth points on their hands and when the applicant reached a three-digit number, the old woman dismissed her and had other expectations from the next person; for example, to sing for her or tell a joke or throw herself to the wall and the floor.

Fernanda told the old woman that she would not have such brutal expectations from the applicant and she had something different in mind.

Again, the old woman congratulated her for being so lucky and said, "You arrived exactly after thirty years of my service. Why sit there, come on because it is your turn as of twelve o'clock."

Fernanda noticed that it was 00:05 AM and five minutes had passed since her service time, so she was a little angry with the old woman because she had to work five more minutes in that day.

Before her departure, the old woman introduced the little girl to her and said, "This little girl is sixty-four. The doctor has manipulated her physiological system so she only ages internally, and you should not be deceived by her diligence and make her work too much, because if she dies, you should find another little girl and it is unclear that the doctor who did that fifty-five years ago is still alive or not. So, do not make her work hard."

Fernanda asked the old woman, "Where are you going now?"

"Maybe I go to die or perhaps to stand in the line. I do not know. I have not made my decision yet," replied the old woman.

Fernanda crossed her legs and called the next applicant with a smile. The petite girl entered. Fernanda asked her about her education and her skills.

The petite girl said, "As I told you, I have a master's degree in sociology and I know how to knit too."

A Country Called the World

"Idiot. When I am here, it means no one is going to be hired for the next thirty years! Ha, ha," said Fernanda sarcastically.

The petite girl was upset and said, "How proud are you of yourself."

Fernanda replied, "It is not my fault. When you are on the path to your goal and realize it would be much harder than what you had thought, your heart breaks, you get upset and cry; and when you achieve your goal and see you are supposed to have much more fun than you had thought, you will automatically feel proud. As if the brain regains its balance by that. Next applicants please!"

The petite girl exited from the back door and for the sake of diversity, Fernanda decided to tell the little girl to go and send in a ten-year worth of all persons in the line, so she could send them out of the back door with a wave of hand without stopping anyone.

The little girl said goodbye and added that she would see her again in the next twenty years. Fernanda ate and slept for ten years. After ten years, the queue restarted. Fernanda was pleased to see the applicants who entered one after the other and exited through the back door. People standing at the end of the queue were very happy to see that the line was moving steadily.

A Country Called the World

Australia

Mesmerized by One's Own Art

After they set a date for the next day, David said, "Thank you for accepting my invitation. I really enjoyed your dance yesterday," and then, when Shirley asked him about his job, he replied, "Theft. I am a thief. I excel at stealing from the elderly houses. I like this specialty so much. It is way easier than stealing from young people and banks and shops. The elderly people often hide their money at home."

Shirley looked at him with bewilderment and with a peal of laughter that clearly exposed her rabbit teeth, gestured that she did not believe him.

"OK, look!" said David.

He got up from his seat and stumbled into the man who was entering the restaurant.

In the blink of an eye, he snatched the man's wallet and showed it to Shirley. In order to show off his power to Shirley, he waited until the man finished eating. The man was desperately looking for his wallet after finishing the meal, however, David went back to him and made body contact with him and put the wallet in its place.

Shirley admired his calm and masculine looks but did not believe him and thought that he was surely going to pull her leg and he was nothing more than just a magician.

A Country Called the World

David laughed and said, "I could be a magician. I make the money disappear from its owner's pocket and reappear in my pocket."

Shirley: "But you do not look like a thief at all."

David: "I grew up with my uncle. He was a wealthy citizen of Sydney, but he never gave me pocket money."

For a moment, he stopped talking about what he was going to say, and said, "Pocket money! Is there anything more important than money in the world! Do you see? Pocket money, savings, loan, rich, poor."

He rubbed his eyes and added, "At all ages, our life is tied with money. I said my uncle did not give me any pocket money at all. I needed it so I could have fun with my friends and eat and most importantly, gain confidence. So, one night, when I was a teenager, I had to take money from his pocket. Do you call it theft?" and immediately added, "No, it is not fair to call it theft! I was beaten the next day but it was worth it. Gradually, I learned how to steal from others. After picking my uncle's pocket, I got acquainted with the art of robbery."

He clinked his glass with that of Shirley's and said, "Cheers to the good old days!" then looked proudly at Shirley which meant, 'Now you tell me about yourself.'

Shirley went on talking to him hoping that she would say goodbye to him forever when she would leave the restaurant.

Therefore, she said, "When I was a child, my parents did not allow me to go to the ballet club. I loved ballet. There was a ballet club at a short distance to our home. As far as I remember, I spent my childhood behind its windows to watch the dance. After I got older, one of my classmates was a ballerina. I learned a lot from her and eventually became a professional. Two years ago, when I was separated from the family, I immediately signed up in the club and just last year, I was recruited in a professional team and this year I will be participating in a number of performances."

"So, in fact, it could be said that you learned ballet by yourself! But I was trained for theft," said David.

Shirley asked as she was getting up from her seat, "Do they teach robbery?!"

David: "Theft requires bravery. I learned it from my uncle."

After leaving the restaurant, David asked, "In your opinion, do you dance better or do I steal better?"

Shirley: "Everyone specializes in a certain field!"

David: "Let me rephrase my question. Imagine both of us are at a scene. You are dancing and I am stealing. Which one attracts the people's attention most? My stealing or your dancing?"

Shirley thought a bit and realized that she had been amazed by David's skillful pick pocketing a few minutes ago and she was sure if someone was dancing there at that moment, she would have still focused on David. Based on such a comparison, ballet seemed to be inferior.

David smiled, "I am even ready to compete with the best dancers and artists. On the one hand, they with their performance, and on the other hand, I wish my art of robbery. I am sure that I will draw all the attention to myself! I was very pleased to meet you. By the way, I am going to steal a little money from an old couple's house tomorrow afternoon. Just a little! Ha, ha! If you like it, I will be waiting for you tomorrow behind this restaurant. Incidentally, a few feet away from the house I am going to rob, there is a house where an old couple lives. So we are equal in that respect! They always leave the house at four o'clock and return home two hours later. Believe me; I have not stolen anything from them until now. I just want to prove to you that if they see you dancing in their house, the first thing that catches their attention is the way you entered the house and not the dance. If you like, I will see you there tomorrow. Have a good day."

Shirley was upset when she reached home, 'Filthy thief! He compares himself with me! I will go with him tomorrow to make him understand that ballet, this pure art, has a special place in the world. I swear even if a ballerina breaks into a house for theft, but begin to dance as soon as the landlord arrives; the landlord would be mesmerized by her moves and absolutely forgets that she has broken into the house."

Then she imagined the landlord's face whose house she was going to the next day, as he would be fascinated by her moves and applauded after the performance and told her, 'You are a wonderful girl!'

The next day, at about five forty, David sneaked Shirley into the aforementioned house and went away to mind his business. Immediately after arriving at the house, Shirley turned on the gramophone and began dancing. Shirley was dancing and David was stealing a necklace and a ring and a lot of money in the bed drawer. When the old couple entered the house jokingly and laughingly, they marveled at a tall and pretty girl who was dancing. Shirley was dancing enthusiastically without paying attention to them, and interestingly, she had her ballet dress on. She finished her dance and looked at the old man and the old lady who looked back at her with astonishment, lowered her head politely, grabbed her clothes and left the house.

She thought to herself as she reached home, 'The next time we meet, he will surely say that they were old and maybe they did not say anything to you because of fear! Ha, ha! Idiot, I am ready to go to any house you choose to prove to you everyone will be mesmerized by my dance and will not pay attention to anything else."

A Country Called the World

A Country Called the World

Argentina

The Brick Wall

The young girl, dressed in a long, white gown, was washing clothes at noon in a house inside a large garden surrounded by high concrete walls. She sang and made faces at the toddlers playing in the water and chased them, oblivious to the eye peeping at her from behind the thin wall of the butcher's shop. As she washed the clothes, her dress's collar was always wide open and at the end, her skirt stuck to her back.

One day, Dennis, a 12-year-old boy who had recently begun working in the newly opened Mr. Ferris butcher's shop, bent over to throw out the carcass of a cockroach that was killed by Mr. Ferris and saw a brick whose color was different than the rest of the bricks, and after he touched it, he realized that the brick was loose in its place. Thanks to his curiosity and power of imagination, Dennis removed the brick from its place (he was eager to hit hidden doors or see a treasure and antique map or some vague item on the floor and the wall). Mr. Ferris was standing at the shop's doorway, talking to one of his friends and could not see Denis from that angle. Dennis made sure that no one was in the shop and bent down and looked at the hollow space of the brick. He did not hit a treasure map, nor a secret button or door, but his heart was thrilled and beat fast, and he thought it was unlikely that what he was expecting to see could excite him so much. His noisy breathing scattered the dust that had spattered the floor after removing the brick and a slight shudder in his body made him realize that he was not concentrated enough to focus on that scene because he did not sit correctly. So, he preferred to lie on his stomach to see well. But he could not do it because he thought the process of backing up, lying down, and looking again, was very long and he had not enough time and may miss the lovely scene in that process. He had a pain in the neck and his shoulders were tired. As he was sat down and bent his head in a way that before that time, he did not know his body was so flexible, and his hands made two narrow and weak bridges between his body and the wall, Mr. Ferris's voice made him to wonderfully retreat in a second. He placed the brick in its place and got up.

– "Hey boy! Where are you?"

Fortunately, Mr. Ferris called him from the doorway. Dennis picked up the mop and immediately went to him.

"Did you completely mop the store?" asked Mr. Ferris.

Dennis: "Yes, sir. Just a little bit is left."

Mr. Ferris: "You and Edward go with Mr. Gomez to help him move. Max, please do not look at him like that. This feeble body can lift the heaviest loads all by itself," he looked back and said, "Edward! Sluggish creep! Hurry!" Edward, who was skinny like Dennis, ran and joined them.

On the way to Mr. Gomez's shop, Edward asked Dennis: "Do you work in the butcher's shop?"

Denis nodded.

Edward said, "You are lucky. I work at the slaughterhouse. Do you know what are we supposed to move?"

This time, Dennis shook his head no.

Edward went to Mr. Gomez who was walking ahead of them and asked, "Excuse me, sir. What are your goods?"

Mr. Gomez understood his question but instead of saying, 'I sell disposable tableware and you must carry as many as you can and bring them from the warehouse to the shop', joked, "I sell ironware!"

At the time of moving the plastic containers, Dennis worked fast and was two rounds ahead of Edward. When Edward saw him working like that, stopped him at the warehouse and said, "Work slower to spend the whole day here. You are happy in your butcher's shop, but I. . . look. Look at my back."

Dennis glanced at him indifferently and regardless of his words, continued to work quickly. He wanted to finish the work as soon as possible to return to the butcher's shop. He did not mind whether he carried ironware or plastic. No matter what it was, he carried it quickly in the same way.

An hour later, Mr. Gomez returned and said with amazement, "Gentlemen! My dears! I did not say carry all I stored in the warehouse to the shop!"

He pointed to four-fifths of the goods and said, "That much should go back to the warehouse."

Edward was pleased and after Mr. Gomez went away, he begged and implored to Dennis, "Slow down! Look! It takes at least two hours and we can finish it in three hours. But I am okay with the damned two hours. By god, please work slowly."

Edward's shaky voice and his face that showed signs of imminent weeping made Dennis reconsider his plea. Shortly after Dennis's departure, Mr. Ferris, in his shop, looked at the brick that was awkwardly put in its place and laughed.

A Country Called the World

In the afternoon, Mr. Ferris dismissed Denis earlier than ever and said, "You got really tired today. It is better to go home, but tomorrow morning come earlier to pack up the meat chops."

That night after dinner, Dennis, without saying a word, lay on his stomach at the corner of the room of their half-ruined house and stared at the opposite wall. His mother slowly went to spread the mattress for him to sleep, and when she saw his puzzled face staring at the opposite wall, her heart sank as usual and thought what could have occupied Dennis's mind to that extent apart from accusing questions like "Why me? Why should I be a working child? Why should I have disabled parents? Why was I born in such a family?"

She thought that no matter how kind and sympathetic she may be to her child, she could not make up for his bad luck and suffering. He needed something more than maternal love and his mother knew it. But she could not ignore the only thing that she could do for her child. So, she went to him and, as always, stroked his head and asked, "Are you okay?"

For the mother, those words always meant: 'Pardon me that you have not experienced anything but hardship since you were born.'

Dennis replied, "Perfect!" without taking his eyes from the wall, and then he faced the ceiling and said, "I have to go earlier tomorrow. Good night, mom."

He yawned and his mother got up and went away. Dennis closed his eyes and turned to the wall behind him. He imagined what if around the whole house, or better, wherever he lay down, a brick wall was before him, and for him, each of the bricks could be easily removed from their places so he would be able to see behind the wall, a girl with long black hair and a headband with a small knot and a delicate body and white dress.

He woke up so early in the morning that to kill the time until having breakfast, he had to mess up with his room and rearrange it again.

Mr. Ferris had gone to the slaughterhouse. From his special chamber, he called Edward and told him, "Today, I am going to bring someone to take your place!"

Edward said, "Sir, please do not do it. I need this job."

Mr. Ferris bent slightly and looked at Edward's face and smiled, "You will come with me to the butcher's shop."

Edward breathed a sigh of relief. He went to the water tap to wash his hands and face and brutally desired to see Dennis working at the slaughterhouse. The slaughterhouse was full of ten to eleven-year-old laborers and was located at a quiet and uncrowned area like the butcher's shop.

As soon as Dennis arrived at the shop, before packing the meat and even before fully pushing up the shop's blinds, went to the wall and removed the brick. He scanned a few pieces of dry clothes that hung on the rope, the slippers and shoes at the top of the stairs, and a three-wheeler that was closest to his eyes and had somewhat blocked his view. He hoped that she would be there around noon. He looked at the shoes again, fearing that the girl may not be at home. Next, to a few pairs of small slippers and a pair of large slippers, he saw a pair of girls' slippers, which in his opinion, was more delicate than the queens' shoes. He put the brick back at its place and hastily began to pack the meat. He had to pack at least ninety pieces of meat till noon. He finished the job two hours before noon. Then, he looked out of the store to make sure Mr. Ferris was not around. He removed the brick from its place and waited to see the girl. His white-clothed mistress had a red brassiere and a black, short skirt on and had just woken up. As she picked up the rope and began to tie it in the yard, Dennis opened his paw to the same size of her boobs and a slight tic ran through his fingers. He wanted to go through the hole in the wall and throw himself on her and touch her all over. He did not notice the passage of time, since an hour that passed while he was still sitting there, by the dull ticking off the clock, turned to a flood of Dennis's sexy thoughts. Moments later, the sound of Mr. Ferris's footsteps was heard which was like an ax cutting a tree. But Dennis was oblivious. Mr. Ferris saw Dennis down on the floor, sticking his eyes to the wall; however, he returned and got out of the shop. He took Edward's hand and pretended that he had dropped something on the floor behind him. Then he went a few steps away from the shop and called Dennis. Dennis immediately got up and put the brick at its place and picked up a pack of meat.

Mr. Ferris entered the shop along with Edward and said, "I brought you a co-worker!"

Edward looked at Dennis proudly.

Mr. Ferris: "Did you pack the meat?"

"Yes, sir," replied Dennis, and immediately went to the fridge and showed the pieces of meat to Mr. Ferris.

Dennis stood behind Mr. Ferris and Edward, and as they looked at the meat packs, he was careful that they, especially Edward, do not see the brick.

A Country Called the World

Mr. Ferris noticed Dennis's angry look at Edward. He grabbed the hands of both of them and took them out of the store and said, "Listen well. If you hate each other, you can beat the hell out of each other outside my shop. But you should be friends inside the shop. Got it? Okay, Dennis, teach the job to Edward. I will be back later and designate the duties of each of you," and as he was leaving the shop, he said, "Edward! Please, do what your co-worker asks. After all, he has been at this place longer than you."

Dennis did not care what Mr. Ferris was saying and instead of being prompted to deal badly with Edward, went inside the shop with Edward and said, "When I come here in the morning, I sweep the floor. Again at night, I have to sweep the floor."

Edward said immediately, "I sweep in the morning and you do it at night." Dennis said, "You need to be very careful not to put your hand in the meat grinder, otherwise your hand will turn to mush. In the past, someone used the chopping knife to cut the meat but mistakenly cut his four fingers!"

Edward picked up the mop and began to work. Dennis immediately snatched it from his hand and said: "No. It is not necessary to mop now."

Edward said, "You have not mopped the store last night, nor now, and now it is a mess."

Dennis realized that Edward was referring to the dust next to the brick wall and began to work.

"It was agreed that I sweep in the morning," Edward said.

"Today, you get some rest. Sit here and see my work," answered Dennis.

A Country Called the World

Throughout that day, Edward saw nothing but sweeping and mopping, and as Dennis told him about the work's risks and hardships - that none of them were true - so that he may get scared and leave the workplace and return to slaughterhouse, Edward pretended that he believed his words and was frightened, but in his heart, he was very pleased with his new job and it did not matter to him that Dennis hated him.

A week passed after Edward's presence and he realized that there was nothing to do but sweeping and packing the meat, so he sarcastically said to Dennis, "Boy, as you sweep, be careful not to fall to the floor and get your brain shattered to pieces!"

He was fed up by asking Dennis with a suspicious face that why they had no customers and only had to pack pieces of meat that the vehicle brought them to the store every day. He persistently said that the shop was a front and it was not known what was embedded in the pieces of meat. Of course, he said this with the mood of a person who knew everything. Dennis never spoke to Edward during that time except for the first day and hated him immensely. Edward tried hard to shake hands of friendship with him but he did not care. During the week that Dennis could not see the white-clothed girl, he was so disturbed and depressed that a week of heavy round-the-clock work could not break him like that. One afternoon, Mr. Ferris took him to mow the lawn of his house and Edward was alone in the butcher's shop, and Dennis had a near-death experience by visualizing Edward peeping at the white-clothed girl.

Mr. Ferris brought both of them out of the butcher's shop and said, "Okay, kids. Wait here!"

A Country Called the World

He entered the butcher's shop and removed the brick from its place. Then he said to Edward, "Pay attention to the work. You must take care of the shop alone till afternoon."

Dennis began mowing the lawn and stressful thoughts rushed to his head as he worked. He imagined Edward peeping through; perhaps he could talk to the white-clothed girl from that spot and befriend her! While thinking about Edward was punishing Dennis, he could imagine himself grabbing Edward's throat and plunging the chopping knife into his face or pounding his head with the same brick a few times. But Edward was far from him. The only thing he could do was to push the lawnmower forward. He was so keen to cut the grass at the root that once the lawnmower's blade hit the ground and made a noise and that caused him to think that if he did not cut the grass properly, the next time Mr. Ferris would take Edward to do it.

The next day, Dennis looked at the brick a few times from the corner of his eye without alarming Edward, and even once, while Edward was packing a few feet away, he sat down and carefully checked the brick. The brick's color seemed so different than the rest of the bricks that Edward should have been extremely dumb not to notice it. But the brick was in the wall as ever and there was not a trace of its displacement. Dennis was thankful that Edward had not seen the brick the previous day. Moments later, Dennis realized Edward was suspiciously silent. He usually poked fun at Dennis at the workplace and regardless of whether Dennis listened to him or not, talked about hard work at the slaughterhouse, his family and his life story. Suddenly, Dennis decided to attack Edward and, by threatening his life, investigate whether he had seen the brick; but he regretted the idea and thought it was a stupid thing to do. Anyway, even if he had peeped through, Dennis's attack would cause Edward to complain of him to Mr. Ferris and Mr. Ferris would become aware of the matter and expel him from the shop. On the other hand, Dennis was not so intimate with Edward and did not consider him an important person worthy of talking to him about his interest in the white-clothed girl, so at a time like the previous day when Edward was alone, he would not peep at the girl. Those thoughts were driving him crazy, so he grabbed the mop and began to clean the floor, hoping that Edward would say, "Hey! Mr. Ferris said we need to pack today."

Edward was packing the meat without paying any attention to him, and said: "Packing! We need to do packing today!"

He said it without looking at Dennis, and though his voice was not as energetic as ever, for Dennis, it was enough to put the mop aside and begin to pack.

As he sat next to Edward, Dennis nudged him happily and said, "I am here!"

He had never talked to Edward like that before. Edward looked at him with surprise and laughed to increase the intimacy, "Are you ready to race?! The one who packs fewer packages must work instead of the winner tomorrow!"

"How dare you say that!" said Dennis with a sparkle in his eyes, "I am ready to work in your stead for ten days and you do not touch anything! To work here is even easier than sitting at home!"

Edward said, "But if the slaughterhouse . . ."

Denis interrupted him and said, "Yes, if we were in a slaughterhouse, that condition made sense!" and nervously repeated several times, "Slaughterhouse, slaughterhouse, slaughterhouse!"

Edward said, "If you were in my shoes, you would never forget that place till the end of your life. Where are you from, by the way? Did I tell you that I am from Bernal?"

"Yes, you said it a hundred times," said Dennis, "I am from Moreno. Okay, I am ready to compete with you!" and flexed his arms for Edward.

Edward: "Are you sure? Let's try."

Then, he lay down on his stomach at the same spot and stuck up his hand. Dennis freaked out at first but then realized Edward was going to arm-wrestle with him and promptly lay down on his stomach in front of him. But when they gripped their hands, Dennis got up and said, "No way. I am not comfortable on this side. Let's switch our places."

Edward thought such excuses have root in Dennis's weakness and felt confident that he would defeat him. But Dennis just wanted to change places to keep the brick out of Edward's field of view. They did not hate each other anymore and as Edward noticed, Dennis nudged him and that paved the way to promote friendship and intimacy between them. But it was crucial for both to defeat the other one in arm-wrestling since both of them thought it was likely that the hostility would erupt again, and perhaps the next confrontation could be more serious and aggressive than the previous one; so much so that they get physical and the more powerful one won. This possibility swelled the veins in the arms and necks of Dennis and Edward and they turned red and shook uncontrollably. Edward lost after a moment of resistance. Dennis got up and felt happy in his heart. He could not imagine defeating Edward like that.

A Country Called the World

Edward, the guy who had become so tough under the heavy workload of the slaughterhouse! But he did not want Edward to feel weak and, because of this defeat, practice so much so that he could win over him. Therefore, he took his hand and lifted him from the floor. They began to work again.

A few days passed, and Dennis was eager to see the white-clothed girl again. He was willing to work hard at the slaughterhouse for a week just to see her again. He was very intimate with Edward but did not want to tell him about it. Edward told him a few times, "I have to tell you a secret," and Dennis, assuming that Edward was going to talk about stealthy work at the slaughterhouse, postponed it to a later time. For Dennis, it did not matter that Mr. Ferris bootlegged whiskey, or owned how many slaughterhouses and casinos and apartments, and so on. Dennis was just interested in how to see the white-clothed girl again from behind the brick wall. One day, he finally made his decision and told Edward, "I want to share a secret with you!"

"I know everything that is related to Mr. Ferris," Said Edward, "Ha, ha, ha."

Dennis said, "It is not related to him."

"So, it cannot be a big deal," said Edward.

"It is about the butcher's shop!" said Dennis.

Edward wondered, "Incidentally, the last secret I wanted to tell you was about his shop!"

Mr. Ferris yelled from outside, "Dennis! Hey, boy!"

Dennis turned away his surprised eyes from Edward's puzzled eyes and went toward Mr. Ferris, who entered the butcher's shop and was cunningly eyeing both of them.

A Country Called the World

Mr. Ferris patted his shoulder hard and said: "Come with me, Edward! Today you have to work on your own!"

Dennis went with Mr. Ferris and looked back as he walked away from the shop. He saw Edward checked the outside for a moment and immediately retreated to the shop. Although heavy work before starting his job at the butcher's shop had improved Dennis's stamina like an adult man, but his heart could not take that much grief and his brain - the same brain that was forced to think about the livelihood problems much earlier than the kids of his age - did not work well at that moment.

It was not a long time after his arrival at Mr. Ferris's house that he decided to run to the shop and check whether Edward had seen the brick and the secret that he was supposed to tell him was not about the brick and related to the bootlegging and slaughterhouse and that sort of cheesy stuff. Mr. Ferris noticed his anxious face and saw that Dennis suddenly jumped up from his place. He ignored his getting up without permission and said, "Hey! I totally forgot about it. After five minutes, go to the shop and fetch a kilo of meat that I have put aside for my home. I will nap for a while. After five minutes."

Dennis realized that he would definitely go there, and explained away his sudden impulse by making excuses about the need to pee.

After five minutes, without wondering why Mr. Ferris had brought him home, Dennis immediately left the house. Other than those five minutes which felt like five centuries to him, the short distance between Mr. Ferris's houses to the shop seemed too long as well. He was panting as he entered the shop. He could not see Edward. He could not find Edward packing the meat behind the refrigerator. If he was there, he could be visible from the front of the shop too. Edward did not notice his presence. Dennis had this strange impulse to grab the large butcher's knife and kill Edward as he was lying down on his stomach, looking at the other side of the wall. He imagined that on the way to the jail, he would speak to the white-clothed girl, saying, "I killed him because of you."

The intense jerks of his heartbeat were enough to scare away all the slaughterhouse's flies! All of a sudden, Edward noticed that someone was in the shop. He jumped to his feet immediately. Without saying a word, Dennis sat down at his place and looked at the other side of the brick wall. The white-clothed girl was washing toddlers' clothing, and her wet dress had stuck to her body and revealed its curves. Denise shuddered. Not because of the scene he saw, but because Edward should not have seen that scene.

Abruptly, he charged Edward like a lion, grasped his neck and pinned down his feeble body to the floor like a thin wooden stick and shouted, "Hands off my love!"

Mr. Ferris entered the shop at that very moment and without demanding any explanations from anybody, grabbed Dennis's shoulder and kicked him out of the shop. Dennis sat a corner and looked at the shop with resentment. On the other hand, Edward read Dennis's angry face and knew he would be back to take revenge for his dismissal sooner or later.

Therefore, as Mr. Ferris was going to leave the shop, he broke the silence and said, "Sir, please do not go anywhere. Dennis thinks I got him fired. He will probably be lying in ambush until you are gone, to come and finish me off. Just send me back to the slaughterhouse again."

A Country Called the World

Mr. Ferris ignored the brick; neither asked Edward why Denis attacked him. "In a couple of days, I will send you to the slaughterhouse again. I hang around, do not be afraid boy," said Mr. Ferris and got out of the shop.

Edward put the brick back at its place and looked at the doorway from his place behind the refrigerator. He was fully alert. As he expected, Denis suddenly rushed into the shop with a long stick in hand. With a battle scream, he attacked Edward.

Everyone knew that Edward threw the Chopping knife toward Dennis to defend himself and he could not be called a murderer. But there was no place in the butcher's shop for him anymore and he had to be imprisoned and tried. Several days later, Mr. Ferris brought another boy to the store and was looking forward to bring him a co-worker from the slaughterhouse, only after the lad saw the other side of the brick wall.

www.ingramcontent.com/pod-product-compliance
Lightning Source LLC
Chambersburg PA
CBHW051816090426
42736CB00011B/1512